Joseph Ritson

Pieces of Ancient Popular Poetry

Joseph Ritson

Pieces of Ancient Popular Poetry

ISBN/EAN: 9783744673723

Printed in Europe, USA, Canada, Australia, Japan

Cover: Foto ©Thomas Meinert / pixelio.de

More available books at **www.hansebooks.com**

PIECES

OF

Ancient Popular Poetry:

FROM

AUTHENTIC MANUSCRIPTS

AND

OLD PRINTED COPIES.

ADORNED WITH CUTS.

To make suche trifels it asketh some counnyng.
                                    SKELTON.

LONDON:

PRINTED BY C. CLARKE,

FOR T. AND J. EGERTON, WHITEHALL.

MDCCXCI.

PREFACE.

THE genius which has been succesfully exerted in contributing to the inſtruction or amuſement of ſociety, in even the rudeſt times, ſeems to have ſome claim upon its gratitude for protection in more enlightened ones. It is a ſuperannuated domestic, whoſe paſsed ſervices entitle his old age to a comfortable proviſion and retreat; or rather, indeed, a humble friend, whoſe attachment in adverſe circumſtances demands the warm and grateful acknowlegements of proſperity. The venerable though nameleſs bards whom the generoſity of the public is now courted to rescue from oblivion and obscurity, have been the favourites of the people for ages, and could once boast a more numerous train of applauding admirers than the most celebrated of our modern poets. Their compositions, it may be true, will have few charms in the critical eye of a cultivated age; but it should always be remembered, that, without such efforts, humble as they are, cultivation or refinement would, never exist, and barbarism and ignorance be eternal. It is to an ENNIUS, perhaps, that we are indebted for a VIRGIL, to such writers as PEELE and GREENE, or others still more obscure, that we owe the admirable dramas of our divinest SHAKSPEARE; and if we are ignorant of the comparatively wretched attempts which called forth the deservedly immortal powers of HOMER or CHAUCER, it is by no means

PREFACE. vii

to be infered that they were the earlyeft of poets, or fprung into the world, as has been faid of the inimitable dramatift already mentioned, like Minerva out of the head of Jupiter, at full growth, and mature.

> *Vixere fortes ante Agamemnona*
> *Multi; fed omnes illacrymabiles*
>   *Urgentur, ignotique longâ*
>   *Noɛte.*

Any enquiry, it is prefumed, after the authors of thefe fugitive productions is at prefent impoffible. It can only be conjectured that they were writen (or, more accurately fpeaking, perhaps, imagined and commited to memory) by men, who made it their profeffion to chant or rehearfe them, up and down the country, in the trophyed hall or before the gloomy caftle, and at marriages, wakes and other feſtive meetings, and who generally accompanyed their ſtrains, by no means ruder than the age itſelf, with the tinkling of a harp, or ſometimes, it is apprehended, with the graces of a much humbler inſtrument. It may, indeed, be conceived that they would now and then be furniſhed with a ſuperior performance from the cloiſter or college; as even the great ſir Thomas More has left us ſomething of the ſame kind*. But, however it was, they ſeem to have been more attentive to temporary applauſe or preſent emolument than to future fame, of which they had poſſibly no idea, and, while they conſigned their effuſions to the caſual protection of an auditors

---

* "A mery ieſt how a ſergeaunt would learne to play the frere. Written in hys youth (for his paſtime)." See his *Workes*, 1557, and the "Hiſtory of the Engliſh language," prefixed to Dr. Johnſons *Dictionary*.

PREFACE. ix

memory, were totally indifferent whether they were remembered or forgoten. The confequence is that while we are indebted for thofe which remain to accident and good fortune, numbers have perifhed, not lefs, and poffibly even more, worthy of prefervation. The reader who wifhes for further information concerning this fet of men may find his curiofity gratifyed by confulting Dr. Percys very ingenious and elegant " Effay on the ancient Englifh Minftrels," prefixed to his " *Reliques of ancient English Poetry,*" and fome " Obfervations" on the fame character in a collection of " *Ancient Songs,*" publifhed by J. Johnfon, in St. Pauls Church-yard*.

* It is fufpected, however, that the prefent copy of the *Hiftory of Tom Thumb* has been modernifed by fome balladwriter of Queen Elizabeths time; very probably the fame Richard Johnfon who afterward turned it into profe.

PREFACE.

It might naturally enough excite the surprise of the intelligent reader, that in a professed republication of popular poetry, nothing should occur upon a subject indisputably the most popular of all—the history of our renowned English archer, ROBIN HOOD. Some apology is undoubtedly necessary on this head, as the omission is by no means owing to ignorance or neglect. In fact, the poems, ballads, and historical or miscellaneous matter, in existence, relative to this celebrated outlaw, are sufficient to furnish the contents of even a couple of volumes considerably bulkyer than the present; and fully deserve to appear in a separate publication, " unmix'd with baser matter."

It would be no trifling gratification to the editor of this little volume, and contribute in some degree, he is persuaded, to the amusement of even the literary part of the public, if the present attempt should be productive of others of a similar nature. Many of our old poems, which would even now be of acknowleged excellence, are scarcely known by name. Such, for instance, are "*The wife lapped in Morels skin, or The taming of a shrew,*" "*The high way to the spittle house,*" "*The schole house of women,*" "*The unlucky firmentie,*" and some others; all or most of which abound with a harmony, spirit, keenness, and natural humour, little to be expected, perhaps, in compositions of so remote a period; and which would by no means appear to have lost their relish. These pieces, indeed, are not only of much greater length than, but of a very different structure from, those in the following collection, and evidently appear to have been written for the prefs. The popularity of the two firſt is evinced by their being mentioned by Laneham (or Langham), in his *Letter ſignifying the Queenz entertainment at Killingwoorth Caſtl*, 1575, along with ſeveral others, among which are ſome of thoſe here printed, as extant in the whimſical but curious library of Captain Cox, a maſon of Coventry, who had " great overſight in matters of ſtorie," and appears to have been a wonderful admirer and collector of old poetry, romances, and ballads.

It is not the editors inclination to enter more at large into the nature or merits of the poems he has here collected. The originals have fallen in his way on various occaſions, and the pleaſing recollection of that happyeſt

PREFACE.

period of which moſt of them were the familiar acquaintance, has induced him to give them to the public with a degree of elegance, fidelity and correctneſs, ſeldom inſtanced in republications of greater importance. Every poem is printed from the authority refered to, with no other intentional licenſe than was occaſioned by the diſuſe of contractions, and a regular ſyſtematical punctuation, or became neceſſary by the errors of the original, which are generally, if not uniformly, noticed in the margin, the emendation being at the ſame time diſtinguiſhed in the text. Under theſe circumſtances, the impreſſion is commited to the patronage of the liberal and the candid, of thoſe whom the artificial refinements of modern taſte have not rendered totally inſenſible to the humble effusions of unpolished nature, and the simplicity of old times; a description of readers, it is to be hoped, sufficiently numerous to justify a wish that it may never fall into the hands of any other.

CONTENTS.

I. ADAM BEL, CLYM OF THE CLOUGHE, AND WYLLYAM OF CLOUDESLE   P. 1

II. A MERY GESTE OF THE FRERE AND THE BOYE 31

III. THE KING AND THE BARKER 57

IV. HOW A MERCHANDE DYD HYS WYFE BETRAY 67

V. HOW THE WISE MAN TAUGHT HIS SON 81

VI. THE LIFE AND DEATH OF TOM THUMBE 93

VII. THE LOVERS QUARREL: OR, CUPIDS TRIUMPH 115

# ADAM BEL,

CLYM OF THE CLOUGHE,

AND

WYLLYAM OF CLOUDESLE.

A

This very ancient, curious, and popular performance, apparently compofed for the purpofe of being fung in public to the harp, is extant in an old quarto, in black letter, without date, " *Imprinted at London in Lothburye by Wyllyam Copland,*" *and preferved among Mr. Garricks Old Plays, now in the Britifh Mufeum, whence it is here given. This copy was made ufe of by Dr. Percy, who has publifhed the poem in his* " *Reliques of Ancient Englifh Poetry,*"* *with fome corrections fortunately fupplyed by another in his folio MS. which may poffibly account for the many different readings between that publication and the prefent. No earlyer edition than Coplands is known. It was reprinted in 1605 by James Roberts, along with* " *The fecond part,*" *a very inferior and fervile production, of which there was, likewife, an edition in 1616, with confiderable variations. Both thefe are in the Bodleian Library.*

As there is no other memorial of thefe celebrated archers than the following legend, to which all the paffages cited, from different authors, by the learned editor already mentioned, are evident allufions, any inquiry as to the time or reality of their exiftence muft be little elfe than the fport of imagination. The paffages refered to are, however, unqueftionable proofs of the great popularity of the poem, which in fact has gone through numberlefs editions; chiefly, it muft be confeffed, in the character of a penny-hiftory.

* *Volume I. p.* 143.

The " *Englishe wood*" *mentioned in v.* 16, &c. *is Englewood or Inglewood, an extensive forest in Cumberland, which was sixteen miles in length, and reached from Carlile to Penrith*. A similar observation has been already made by Dr. Percy, who adds, that* " *Engle or Ingle-wood signifies wood for firing.*" *But, with submission to so good a judge, it should rather seem, in the present instance, to design a wood or forest in which extraordinary fires were made on particular occasions; a conjecture which will appear the more plausible, when it is considered that the identical spot on which Penrith beacon now stands, and where a beacon has stood for ages, was formerly within the limits of this very forest* †; *and that Ingleborough, one of* " *the highest hills between Scotland and Trent,*" *has obtained this name from the fires anciently lighted in the beacon erected on its flat top, where the foundation is still visible.*

" *Clym of the Clough*" *is properly explained by the above ingenious editor to mean* Clem *or* Clement of the Valley. " *Cloudeslè*," *of which the etymology has not been hitherto attempted, may be thought to signify a rocky pasture; from* clud, rupes, *and* leag, pascuum. *See Lyes Saxon Dictionary.*

---

* *Edward the First, in hunting in this forest, is said to have killed two hundred bucks in one day. See the Additions to* Cumberland, *in Camdens Britannia,* 1695.

† *Ibi. and Burns Cumberland, p.* 396.

M ERY it was in grene foreſt,
Amonge the leues grene,
Wher that men walke eaſt and weſt,
Wyth bowes and arrowes kene,
To ryſe the dere out of theyr denne,   5
Such ſightes hath ofte bene ſene,
As by 'thre' yemen of the north countrey,
By them it is I meane:
The one of them hight Adam Bel,
The other Clym of the Clough,   10
The thyrd was William of Cloudeſly,
An archer good ynough.

V. 6. as hath.   *V.* 7. the.   *V.* 8. as I.

They were outlawed for venyſon,
Theſe yemen everechone;
They ſwore them brethren upon a day,   15
To Englyſshewood for to gone.
Now lith and lyſten, gentylmen,
That of myrthes loveth to here:
Two of them were ſingle men,
The third had a wedded fere;   20
Wyllyam was the wedded man,
Muche more then was hys care,
He ſayde to hys brethren upon a day,
To Carelel he would fare.
For to ſpeke with fayre Alſe hys wife,   25
And with hys chyldren thre.
By my trouth, ſayde Adam Bel,
Not by the counſell of me;
For if ye go to Caerlel, brother,
And from thys wylde wode wende,   30
If the juſtice mai you take,
Your lyfe were at an ende.
If that I come not to morowe, brother,
By pryme to you agayne,
Truſte not els but that I am take,   35
Or elſe that I am ſlayne.
He toke hys leaue of hys brethren two,
And to Carlel he is gon,
There he knocked at hys owne windowe,
Shortlye and anone.   40

V. 18. And that.

Where be you, fayre Alyce my wyfe?
And my chyldren three?
Lyghtly let in thyne owne hufbande,
Wyllyam of Cloudeſle.
Alas! then fayde fayre Alyce, 45
And fyghed wonderous fore,
Thys place hath ben befette for you,
Thys half yere and more.
Now am I here, fayde Cloudeſle,
I woulde that I in were;— 50
Now feche us meate and drynke ynoughe,
And let us make good chere.
She fetched hym meat and drynke plenty,
Lyke a true wedded wyfe,
And pleafed hym wyth that ſhe had, 55
Whome ſhe loued as her lyfe.
There lay an old wyfe in that place,
A lytle befyde the fyre,
Whych Wyllyam had found of cherytye
More then feuen yere; 60
Up ſhe rofe and walked full ſtyll,
Euel mote ſhe fpede therefoore,
For ſhe had not fet no fote on ground
In feuen yere before.
She went vnto the juſtice hall, 65
As faſt as ſhe could hye;
Thys nyght is come vnto this town
Wyllyam of Cloudeſle.

V. 41. your.   *V.* 50. In woulde.   *V.* 62. fpende.

Thereof the iustice was full fayne,
And so was the shirife also;   70
Thou shalt not trauaile hether, dame, for nought,
Thy meed thou shalt haue or thou go.
They gaue to her a ryght good goune,
Of scarlat it was as I heard ‘fayne,’
She toke the gyft and home she wente,   75
And couched her downe agayne.
They rysed the towne of mery Carlel,
In all the hast that they can,
And came thronging to Wyllyames house,
As fast as they myght gone.   80
Theyr they besette that good yeman,
Round about on euery syde,
Wyllyam hearde great noyse of folkes,
That heyther ward they hyed.
Alyce opened a ‘shot’ wyndow,   85
And loked all about,
She was ware of the iustice and shirife bothe,
Wyth a full great route.
Alas! treason! cry'd Aleyce,
Euer wo may thou be!   90
‘Go’ into my chambre, my husband, she sayd,
Swete Wyllyam of Cloudesle.

V. 71. fore.
V. 74. faye. *Percy reads* Of scarlate and of graine.
V. 85. shop. *Percy reads* back window.
V. 88. great full great.
V. 91. Gy.

He toke hys fweard and hys bucler,
Hys bow and hy[s] chyldren thre,
And wente into hys ſtrongeſt chamber, 95
Where he thought fureſt to be.
Fayre Alice folowed him as a lover true,
With a pollaxe in her hande;
He ſhal be dead that here cometh in
Thys dore whyle I may ſtand. 100
Cloudeſle bent a wel good bowe,
That was of truſty tre,
He ſmot the juſtife on the breſt,
That hys arrowe breſt in thre.
Gods curſe on his hartt, faide William, 105
Thys day thy cote dyd on,
If it had ben no better then myne,
It had gone nere thy bone.
Yelde the Cloudeſle, ſayd the juſtife,
And thy bowe and thy arrowes the fro. 110
Gods curſe on hys hart, ſayde fair Alce,
That my huſband councelleth ſo.
Set fyre on the houſe, faide the ſherife,
Syth it wyll no better be,
And brenne we therin William, he ſaide, 115
Hys wyfe and chyldren thre.
They fyred the houſe in many a place,
The fyre flew vp on hye;
Alas! then cryed fayr Alice,
I ſe we here ſhall dy. 120

William openyd hys backe wyndow,
That was in hys chambre on hye,
And wyth fhetes let hys wyfe downe,
And hys chyldren thre.
Have here my treafure, fayde William,   125
My wyfe and my chyldren thre,
For Chriftes loue do them no harme,
But wreke you all on me.
Wyllyam fhot fo wonderous well,
Tyll hys arrowes were all gon,   130
And the fyre fo faft vpon hym fell,
That hys bowftryng brent in two.
The fpercles brent and fell hym on,
Good Wyllyam of Cloudefle!
But than wax he a wofull man,   135
And fayde, thys is a cowardes death to me.
Leuer I had, fayde Wyllyam,
With my fworde in the route to renne,
Then here among myne ennemyes wode,
Thus cruelly to bren.   140
He toke hys fweard and hys buckler,
And among them all he ran,
Where the people were moft in prece,
He fmot downe many a man.
There myght no man ftand hys ftroke,   145
So ferfly on them he ran;
Then they threw wyndowes and dores on him,
And fo toke that good yeman.

V. 122. was on.

There they hym bounde both hand and fote,
And in depe dongeon hym caft;   150
Now, Cloudefle, fayd the hye juftice,
Thou fhalt be hanged in haft.
One vow fhal I make, fayde the fherife,
A payre of new galowes fhall I for the make,
And the gates of Caerlel fhal be fhutte,   155
There fhall no man come in therat.
Then fhall not helpe Clim of the Cloughe,
Nor yet fhall Adam Bell,
Though they came with a thoufand mo,
Nor all the deuels in hell.   160
Early in the mornyng the juftice vprofe,
To the gates firft gan he gon,
And commaundede to be fhut full cloce
Lightile everychone.
Then went he to the market place,   165
As faft as he coulde hye,
A payre of new gallous there dyd he vp fet,
Befyde the pyllory.
A lytle boy ftod them amonge,
And afked what meaned that gallow tre ; 170
They fayde, to hange a good yeaman,
Called Wyllyam of Cloudefle.
That lytle boye was the towne fwyne heard,
And kept ' fayre' Alyce fwyne,
Oft he had feene Cloudefle in the wodde,   175
And geuen hym there to dyne.

V. 174. there.

He went out att a creues in the wall,
And lightly to the wood dyd gone,
There met he with thefe wight yonge men,
Shortly and anone.   180
Alas! then fayde that lytle boye,
Ye tary here all to longe;
Cloudeſle is taken and dampned to death,
All readye for to honge.
Alas! then fayde good Adam Bell,   185
That ever we fee thys daye!
He myght her with vs have dwelled,
So ofte as we dyd him praye!
He myght have taryed in grene forefte,
Under the ſhadowes ſheene,   190
And have kepte both hym and vs in reafte,
Out of trouble and teene!
Adam bent a ryght good bow,
A great hart fone had he ſlayne,
Take that, chylde, he fayde to thy dynner, 195
And bryng me myne arrowe agayne.
Now go we hence, fayed thefe wight yong men,
Tary we no lenger here;
We ſhall hym borowe, by gods grace,
Though we bye it full dere.   200
To Caerlel went thefe good yemen,
On a mery mornyng of Maye.
Here is a fyt of Cloudeſli,
And another is for to faye.

V. 201. Cyerlel.

[THE SECOND FIT.]

AND when they came to mery Caerlell,
In a fayre mornyng tyde, 205
They founde the gates shut them vntyll,
Round about on euery syde.
Alas! than fayd good Adam Bell,
That euer we were made men! 210
These gates be shut so wonderous wel,
That we may not come here in.
Then spake him Clym of the Clough,
Wyth a wyle we wyl vs in bryng;
Let vs saye we be meffengers, 215.
Streyght come nowe from our king.
Adam faid, I haue a letter written wel,
Now let us wyfely werke,
We wyl faye we haue the kinges feales,
I holde the portter no clerke. 220
Then Adam Bell bete on the gate,
With strokes great and strong,
The porter herde fuche noyfe therat,
And to the gate he throng.
Who is there nowe, fayde the porter, 225
That maketh all thys knocking?
We be tow meffengers, fayde Clim of the Clough,
Be come ryght from our kyng.

We haue a letter, fayd Adam Bel,
To the juftice we muft it bryng;   230
Let vs in our meffag to do,
That we were agayne to our kyng.
Here commeth none in, fayd the porter,
Be hym that dyed vpon a tre,
Tyll a falfe thefe be hanged,   235
Called Wyllyam of Cloudefle.
Then fpake the good yeman Clym of the Clough,
And fwore by Mary fre,
And if that we ftande longe wythout,
Lyke a thefe hanged fhalt thou be.   240
Lo here we haue the kynges feale;
What! lordeyne, art thou wode?
The porter went it had ben fo,
And lyghtly dyd of hys hode.
Welcome be my lordes feale, he faide,   245
For that ye fhall come in.
He opened the gate full fhortlye,
An euyl openyng for him.
Now are we in, fayde Adam Bell,
Thereof we are full faine,   250
But Chrift know[s], that harowed hell,
How we fhall com out agayne.
Had we the keys, faid Clim of the Clough,
Ryght wel then fhoulde we fpede;
Then might we come out wel ynough,   255
When we fe tyme and nede.

V. 230. me.   *V*. 254. fhaulde.

They called the porter to counſell,
And wrange hys necke in two,
And caſte him in a depe dongeon,
And toke hys keys hym fro.   260
Now am I porter, ſayde Adam Bel,
Se brother the keys haue we here,
The worſt porter to merry Caerlel,
That ye had thys hundred yere:
And now wyll we our bowes bend,   265
Into the towne wyll we go,
For to delyuer our dere brother,
That lyueth in care and wo.
They bent theyr bowes,
And loked theyr ſtringes were round,   270
The market place in mery Caerlel,
They beſet that ſtound;
And as they loked them beſyde,
A paire of new galowes ther thei ſee,
And the juſtice with a queſt of ſquyers,   275
That had judged Cloudeſle there hanged to be:
And Cloudeſle hymſelfe lay redy in a carte,
Faſt both fote and hand,
And a ſtronge rop about hys necke,
All readye for to hange.   280
The juſtice called to him a ladde,
Cloudeſle clothes ſhould he haue,
To take the meaſure of that yeman,
And therafter to make hys graue.

V. 275, they.

I have feen as great a mearveile, faid Cloudeſlī,
As betwyene thys and pryme,
He that maketh thys graue for me,
Himfelfe may lye therin.
Thou fpeakeſt proudli, faide the juſtice,
I ſhall the hange with my hande: 290
Full wel herd hys brethren two,
There ſtyll as they dyd ſtande.
Then Cloudeſle caſt hys eyen afyde,
And faw hys to brethren,
At a corner of the market place,   295
With theyr good bows bent in ther hand,
Redy the juſtice for to chaunce.
I fe comfort, fayd Cloudeſle,
Yet hope I well to fare;
If I might haue my handes at wyll,
Ryght lytle wolde I care.   · 300
Then fpake good Adam Bell,
To Clym of the Clough fo free,
Brother, fe ye marke the juſtyce wel,
Lo yonder ye may him fee;
And at the ſhyr[i]fe ſhote I wyll,   305
Strongly with arrowe kene,
A better ſhote in mery Caerlel
Thys feuen yere was not fene.

V. 293. Claudeſle.   *V.* 294. brethen,
V. 295. marked.   *V.* 298. will.

They lowfed 'their' arrowes both at once,
Of no man had 'they' dread,   310
The one hyt the juftice, the other the fheryfe,
That both theyr 'fides' gan blede.
All men voyded that them ftode nye,
When the juftice fell downe to the grounde,
And the fherife fell nyghe hym by,   315
Eyther had his deathes wounde.
All the citezens faft gan flye,
They durft no longer abyde,
They lyghtly 'then' loufed Cloudcfle,
Where he with ropes lay tyde.   320
Wyllyam fterte to an officer of the towne,
Hys axe out of hys hande he wronge,
On eche fyde he fmote them downe,
Hym thought he taryed all to long.
Wyllyam fayde to hys brethren two,   325
Thys daye let us lyue and dye,
If euer you have nede as I haue now,
The fame fhall you fynde by me.
They fhot fo well in that tyde,
For theyr ftringes were of filke ful fure, 330
That they kept the ftretes on euery 'fide!'
That batayle dyd longe endure.
The[y] fought together as brethren tru,
Lyke hardy men and bolde,
Many a man to the ground they thrue,   335
And many a herte made colde.

V. 309. thre.   *V*. 312. fedes.   *V*. 319. they.
V. 325. brethen.   *V*. 331. fede.   *V*. 336. made many a herte.

B

But when their arrowes were all gon,
Men preced to them full fast,
They drew theyr fwordes then anone,
And theyr bowes from them cast.   340
They went lyghtlye on theyr way,
Wyth fwordes and buclers round,
By that it 'was' myd of the day,
They made mani a wound.
There was an out horne in Caerlel blowen, 345
And the belles bacward did ryng;
Many a woman fayd alas!
And many theyr handes dyd wryng.
The mayre of Caerlel forth com was,
And with hym a ful great route,   350
Thefe yemen dred him full fore,
For of theyr lyues they ftode in great doute.
The mayre came armed a full great pace,
With a pollaxe in hys hande,
Many a ftrong man wyth him was,   355
There in that ftowre to ftande.
The mayre fmot at Cloudlefle with his bil,
Hys bucler he bruft in two,
Full many a yeman with great euyll,
Alas! treafon! they cryed for wo.   360
Kepe we the gates faft they bad,
That thefe traytours thereout not go.
But al for nought was that the[y] wrought,
For 'fo' faft they downe were layde,

V. 343. mas.   *V.* 364. to.

Tyll they all thre, that so manfulli fought, 365
Were gotten without abraide.
Haue here your keys, sayd Adam Bel,
Myne off[i]ce I here forsake,
Yf you do by my councell,
A new porter do ' ye' make. 370
He threw theyr keys at theyr heads,
And bad them euell to thryue,
And all that letteth any good yeman
To come and comfort hys wyfe.
Thus be these good yemen gon to the wod, 375
And lyghtly as ' lefe' on lynde,
The[y] lough an[d] be mery in theyr mode,
Theyr ennemyes were fer[r]e behynd.
When they came to Englyshe wode,
Under the trusty tre, 380
They found bowes full good,
And arrowes full great plentye.
So god me help, s[a]yd Adam Bell,
And Clym of the Clough so fre,
I would we were in mery Caerlel, 385
Before that fayre meyny.
They set them downe and made good chere,
And eate and drynke full well.
Here is a fet of these wyght yong men,
An other I wyll you tell. 390

V. 368, 369. *misplaced in the old edition.*
V. 370. we.   *V.* 376. left.

[THE THIRD FIT.]

As they fat in Englyfhe wood
   Under theyr trufty tre,
They thought they herd a woman wepe,
   But her they mought not fe.
Sore then fyghed the fayre Alyce,   395
   And fayde, alas! that euer I fawe thys daye!
For now is my dere hufband flayne,
   Alas! and wel a way!
Myght I have fpoken wyth hys dere brethren,
   Or with eyther of them twayne,   400
[To let them know what him befell]
   My hart were put out of payne!
Cloudefle walked a lytle befyde,
   And loked vnder the grenewood linde,
He was ware of hys wife and chyldren thre, 405
   Full wo in hart and mynde.
Welcome wife, then fayde Wyllyam,
   Under 'this' trufti tre;
I had wende yefterday, by fwete faynt John,
   Thou fhulde me never 'have' fe.   410

V. 393. thaught.   *V.* 399. brethen:
V. 401. *fupplyed from a modern edition.*
V. 408. thus.   *V.* 410. had.

Now well is me, she sayde, that ye be here,
My hart is out of wo.
Dame, he sayde, be mery and glad,
And thanke my brethren two.
Hereof to speake, sayd Adam Bell,   415
I wis it is no bote;
The meat that we must supp withall
It runneth yet fast on fote.
Then went they down into a launde,
These noble archares all thre,   420
Eche of them flew a hart of greece,
The best they could there se.
Haue here the best, Al[y]ce my wyfe,
Sayde Wyllyam of Cloudesle,
By cause ye so bouldly stod by me,   425
When I was slayne full nye.
Then went they to supper,
Wyth suche meat as they had,
And thanked god of ther fortune,
They were both mery and glad.   430
And when they had supped well,
Certayne without any leace,
Cloudesle sayd, we wyll to our kyng,
To get vs a charter of peace;
Alce shal be at our soiournyng,   435
In a nunry here besyde,
My tow sonnes shall wyth her go,
And ther they shall abyde:

V. 414. brethen.   *V.* 421. gracce.   *V.* 427. whent.

Myne eldeſt ſon ſhall go wyth me,
For hym haue I no care, 440
And he ſhall you breng worde agayn
How that we do fare.
Thus be theſe yemen to London gone,
As faſt as they might hye,
Tyll they came to the kynges pallace, 445
Where they woulde nedes be.
And whan they came to the kynges courte,
Unto the pallace gate,
Of no man wold they aſke no leave,
But boldly went in therat; 450
They preced preſtly into the hall,
Of no man had they dreade,
The porter came after and dyd them call,
And with them began to chyde.
The uſher ſayed, yemen, what wold ye haue? 455
I pray you tell me;
You myght thus make offycers ſhent:
Good ſyrs of whence be ye?
Syr we be out lawes of the foreſt,
Certayne without any leace, 460
And hether we be come to our kyng,
To get vs a charter of peace.
And whan they came before the kyng,
As it was the lawe of the lande,
The[y] kneled downe without lettyng, 465
And eche helde vp his hand.

The[y] fayed, lord we befeche the here,
That ye wyll graunt vs grace,
For we haue flaine your fat falow der,
In many a fondry place.   470
What be your nam[e]s? than faid our king,
Anone that you tell me.
They fayd, Adam Bel, Clim of the Clough,
And Wyllyam of Cloudefle.
Be ye thofe theues, then fayd our kyng, 475
That men haue tolde of to me?
Here to god I make a vowe,
Ye fhal be hanged al thre;
Ye fhal be dead without mercy,
As I am kynge of this lande.   480
He commanded his officers everichone
Faft on them to lay hand.
There they toke thefe good yemen,
And arefted them all thre.
So may I thryue, fayd Adam Bell,   485
Thys game lyketh not me.
But, good lorde, we befeche you now,
That you graunt vs grace,
Infomuche as we be to you comen,
Or els that we may fro you paffe,   490
With fuche weapons as we haue here,
Tyll we be out of your place;
And yf we lyue this hundreth yere,
We wyll afke you no grace.

Ye fpeake proudly, fayd the kynge, 495
Ye fhal be hanged all thre.
That were great pitye, then fayd the quene,
If any grace myght be.
My lorde, whan I came fyrft into this lande,
To be your wedded wyfe, 500
The fyrft bowne that I wold afke,
Ye would graunt it me belyfe;
And I afked neuer none tyll now,
Therefore, good lorde, graunt it me.
Now afke it, madam, fayd the kynge, 505
And graunted fhall it be.
Then, good my lord, I you befeche,
Thefe yemen graunt ye me.
Madame, ye myght have afked a bowne,
That fhuld have ben worth them all three: 510
Ye myght have afked towres and towne[s],
Parkes and foreftes plenty.
None foe pleafaunt to mi pay, fhe faid,
Nor none fo lefe to me.
Madame, fith it is your defyre, 515
Your afkyng graunted fhal be;
But I had leuer have geuen you
Good market townes thre.
The quene was a glad woman,
And fayd, lord, gramarcy, 520
I dare undertake for them
That true men fhal they be.

But, good lord, fpeke fom mery word,
That comfort they may fe.
I graunt you grace, then faid our king,   525
Wafshe, felos, and to meate go ye.
They had not fetten but a whyle,
Certayne without lefynge,
There came meffengers out of the north,
With letters to our kyng.   530
And whan the came before the kynge,
They kneled downe vpon theyr kne,
And fayd, lord, your offycers grete you wel,
Of Caerlel in the north cuntre.
How fare my juftice, fayd the kyng,   535
And my fherife alfo?
Syr, they be flayne, without leafynge,
And many an officer mo.
Who hath them flayne? fayd the kyng,
Anone thou tell me.   540
Adam Bel, and Clime of the Clough,
And Wyllyam of Cloudefle.
Alas! for rewth! then fayd our kynge,
My hart is wonderous fore,
I had leuer [th]an a thoufand pounde,   545
I had knowne of thys before;
For I have graunted them grace,
And that forthynketh me,
But had I knowne all thys before,
They had been hanged all thre.   550

The kyng opened the letter anone,
Hymſelfe he red it tho,
And founde how theſe thre outlawes had ſlaine
Thre hundred men and mo;
Fyrſt the juſtice and the ſheryfe, 555
And the mayre of Caerlel towne,
Of all the conſtables and catchipolles
Alyue were left not one;
The baylyes and the bedyls both,
And the ſergeauntes of the law, 560
And forty foſters of the fe,
Theſe outlawes had yſlaw;
And broke his parks, and ſlaine his dere,
Ouer all they choſe the beſt,
So perelous out lawes as they were, 565
Walked not by eaſte nor weſt.
When the kynge this letter had red,
In hys harte he ſyghed ſore,
Take vp the table anone he bad,
For I may eate no more. 570
The kyng called hys beſt archars,
To the buttes wyth hym to go;
I wyll ſe theſe felowes ſhote, he ſayd,
In the north haue wrought this wo.
The kynges bowmen buſke them blyue, 575
And the quenes archers alſo,
So dyd theſe thre wyght yemen,
With them they thought to go.

There twyfe or thryfe they fhote about,
For to affay theyr hande, 580
There was no fhote thefe yemen fhot,
That any prycke myght them ftand.
Then fpake Wyllyam of Cloudefle,
By him that for me dyed,
I hold hym neuer no good archar 585
That fhuteth at buttes fo wyde.
Wherat? then fayd our kyng,
I pray thee tell me.
At fuche a but, fyr, he fayd,
As men vfe in my countree. 590
Wyllyam went into a fyeld,
And his to brethren with him,
There they fet vp to hafell roddes,
Twenty fcore paces betwene.
I hold him an archar, faid Cloudefle, 595
That yonder wande cleueth in two.
Here is none fuche, fayd the kyng,
Nor none that can fo do.
I fhall affaye, fyr, fayd Cloudefle,
Or that I farther go. 600
Cloudefly, with a bearyng arow,
Claue the wand in to.
Thou art the beft archer, then faid the king,
Forfothe that euer I fe.
And yet for your loue, fayd Wylliam, 605
I wyll do more mayftry:

V. 587. At what a butte now wold ye fhot. *Reliques.*

I haue a fonne is feuen yere olde,
He is to me full deare,
I wyll hym tye to a ftake,
All fhall fe that be here,   610
And lay an apele vpon hys head,
And go fyxe fcore paces hym fro,
And I myfelfe, with a brode arow,
Shall cleue the apple in two.
Now hafte the, then fayd the kyng,   615
By him that dyed on a tre,
But yf thou do not as thou ' haft' fayde,
Hanged fhalt thou be.
And thou touche his head or gowne,
In fyght that men may fe,   620
By all the fayntes that be in heaven,
I fhall hange you all thre.
That I haue promifed, faid William,
I wyl it neuer forfake,
And there euen before the kynge,   625
In the earth he droue a ftake,
And bound therto his eldeft fonne,
And bad hym ftande ftyll therat,
And turned the childes face fro him,
Becaufe he fhuld not fterte;   630
An apple vpon his head he fet,
And then his bowe he bent,
Syxe fcore paces they were out met,
And thether Cloudefle went;

V. 617. heft.

There he drew out a fayr brode arrowe,   635
Hys bowe was great and longe,
He fet that arrowe in his bowe,
That was both ftyffe and ftronge ;
He prayed the people that was there,
That they would ftyll ftande,   640
For he that fhooteth for fuch a wager,
Behoueth a ftedfaft hand.
Muche people prayed for Cloudefle,
That hys lyfe faued myght be,
And whan he made hym redy to fhote,   645
There was many a weping eye.
Thus Cloudefle clefte the apple in two,
That many a man myght fe ;
Ouer gods forbode, fayde the kinge,
That thou fhote at me !   650
I geve the xviii. pence a day,
And my bowe fhalt thou beare,
And ouer all the north countre,
I make the chyfe rydere.
And I geve the xvii. pence a day, faid the quene,
By god and by my fay,   656
Come feche thy payment when thou wylt,
No man fhall fay the nay.
Wyllyam, I make the a gentelman,
Of clothyng and of fe,   660
And thi two brethren yemen of my chambre,
For they are fo femely to fe ;

V. 648, Percy, inftead of this line, reads
His fonne he did not fee.

Your fonne, for he is tendre of age,
Of my wyne feller fhall he be,
And whan he commeth to mannes eftate, 665
Better auaunced fhall he be.
And, Wylliam, bring me your wife, faid the quene,
Me longeth her fore to fe,
She fhal be my chefe gentelwoman,
To gouerne my nurfery. 670
The yemen thanketh them full curteoufly,
And fayde, to fome byfshop wyl we wend,
Of all the fynnes that we have done
To be affoyld at his hand.
So forth be gone thefe good yemen, 675
As faft as they myght hye,
And after came and dwelled wyth the kynge,
And dyed good men all thre.
Thus endeth the liues of thefe good yemen,
God fend them eternall blyffe! 680
And all that with hande bowe fhoteth,
That of heauen may neuer myffe!

A

MERY GESTE

OF

THE FRERE AND THE BOYE.

This well-known tale is furnished, in its present dress, by a copy in the public library of the univerſity of Cambridge, " Enprynted at London in Flete ſtrete at the ſygne of the ſonne by Wynkyn de Worde;" compared with a later edition in the Bodleian library, " Imprinted at London at the long ſhop adioyning vnto Saint Mildreds Church in the Pultrie by Edwarde Alde;" both in quarto and black letter, and of ſingular rarity, no duplicate of either being known to exiſt *. There is, indeed, a very old, though at the ſame time a moſt vulgar and corrupted copy extant in the firſt of thoſe libraries (MSS. More, Ee. 4. 35.) under the title of " The Cheylde and hes ſtep-dame," of which, beſides that almoſt every line exhibits a various reading, the concluding ſtanzas are entirely different, and have, on that account, been thought worth preſerving. But the moſt ancient copy of all would probably have been one in the Cotton library, if the volume which contained it had not unfortunately periſhed, with many things of greater importance, in the dreadful fire which happened in that noble repoſitory, anno 1731. Vide Smiths Catalogue, Vitellius D. XII.

* There was once a copy of one or other of the above editions, or ſome different impreſſion, with divers other curious pieces, in the printed library of Anthony à Wood (No. 66); but the article, with others of the like nature, appears to have been clandeſtinely taken out.

From the mention made in v. 429 of the city of "Orlyaunce," and the character of the "Offycyal," it may be conjectured that this poem is of French extraction; and, indeed, it is not at all improbable that the original is extant in some collection of old Fabliaux. A punishment similar to that of the good wife in this story appears to have been inflicted on the widow of a St. Gengulph, for presuming to question the reality of her husbands miracles. See Heywoods History of Women, p. 196.

The cut prefixed is an exact copy of one in the title of the most ancient edition, which, the present editor has a melancholy pleasure in reflecting, was traced for this purpose by his learned, ingenious, and valuable friend, the late *John Baynes* esquire.

G OD that dyed for vs all,
And dranke both eyfell and gall,
Brynge vs out of bale,
And gyue them good lyfe and longe
That lyfteneth to my fonge, 5
Or tendeth to my tale.
There dwelled an hufbonde in my countre
That had wyues thre,
By proceffe of tyme,
By the fyrft wyfe a fone he had, 10
That was a good fturdy ladde,
And an happy hyne.

His fader loued hym wele,
So dyde his moder neuer a dele,
I tell you as I thinke ; 15
All fhe thought was loft, by the rode,
That dyde the lytell boye ony good,
Other mete or drynke.
And yet y wys it was but badde,
And therof not halfe ynough he had, 20
But euermore of the worfte :
Therfore euyll mote fhe fare,
For euer fhe dyde the lytell boye care,
As ferforth as fhe dorfte.
The good wyfe to her hufbonde gan faye, 25
I wolde ye wolde put this boye awaye,
And that ryght foone in hafte ;
Truly he is a curfed ladde,
I wolde fome other man hym had,
That wolde hym better chafte. 30
Then fayd the good man agayne,
Dame, I fhall to the fayne,
He is but tender of age ;
He fhall abyde with me this yere,
Tyll he be more ftrongere, 35
For to wynne better wage.
We haue a man, a ftoute freke,
That in the felde kepeth our nete,
Slepynge all the daye,
He fhall come home, fo god me fhelde, 40
And the boye fhall into the felde,
To kepe our beeftes yf he may.

Than fayd the wyfe, verament,
Therto foone I affent,
For that me thynketh mooft nedy.   45
On the morowe whan it was daye,
The lytell boye wente on his waye,
To the felde full redy;
Of no man he had no care,
But fung, hey howe, awaye the mare,* 50
And made ioye ynough;
Forth he wente, truly to fayne,
Tyll he came to the playne,
Hys dyner forth he drough:
Whan he fawe it was but bad,   55
Ful lytell luft therto he had,
But put it vp agayne;
Therfore he was not to wyte,
He fayd he wolde ete but lyte,
Tyll nyght that he home came.   60
And as the boye fate on a hyll,
An olde man came hym tyll,
Walkynge by the waye;
Sone, he fayde, god the fe.
Syr, welcome mote ye be,   65
The lytell boye gan faye.

---

* *This seems to have been the beginning or title of some old ballad. Mayſtres Jyll of Brentford takes notice of it in her* " *Teſtament.*" *4to. b. l.*
  "Ah fyrra, mary a way the mare."
V. 60. came home. *De W.*

The olde man fayd, I am an hongred fore,
Haft thou ony mete in ftore,
That thou mayft gyue me?
The chylde fayd, fo god me faue, 70
To fuch vytayle as I haue
Welcome fhall ye be.
Therof the olde man was gladde,
The boye drewe forth fuche as he had,
And fayd, do gladly. 75
The olde man was eafy to pleafe,
He ete and made hym well at eafe,
And fayd, fone, gramercy.
Sone, thou hafte gyuen mete to me,
I fhall the gyue thynges thre, 80
Thou fhalt them neuer forgete.
Than fayd the boye, as I trowe,
It is beft that I haue a bowe,
Byrdes for to ' fhete.'
A bowe, fone, I fhall the gyue, 85
That fhall laft the all thy lyue,
And euer a lyke mete,
Shote therin whan thou good thynke,
For yf thou fhote and wynke,
The prycke thow fhalte hytte. 90
Whan he the bowe in honde felte,
And the boltes vnder his belte,
Lowde than he lough;

V. 84. fhote. *De W.* fhoote. *A.*

He fayd, now had I a pype,
Though it were neuer fo lyte, 95
Than were I gladde ynough.
A pype, fone, thou fhalte haue alfo,
In true mufyke it fhall go,
I put thee out of doubt;
All that may the pype here 100
Shall not themfelfe ftere,
But laugh and lepe aboute.
What fhall the thyrde be?
For I wyll gyue the gyftes three,
As I haue fayd before. 105
The lytell boye on hym lough,
And fayd, fyr, I haue ynough,
I wyll defyre no more.
The olde man fayd, my trouth I plyght,
Thou fhalte haue that I the hyght; 110
Say on now and let me fe.
Than fayd the boye anone,
I haue a ftepdame at home,
She is a fhrewe to me:
Whan my fader gyueth me mete, 115
She wolde theron that I were cheke,
And ftareth me in the face;
Whan fhe loketh on me fo,
I wolde fhe fholde let a rappe go,
That it myght rynge ouer all the place. 120

V. 99. I do the well to wyte. *De W.*
V. 105. to the before. *Idem.*

Than fayd the olde man tho,
Whan fhe loketh on the fo
She fhall begyn to blowe;
All that euer it may here
Shall not themfelfe ftere, 125
But laugh on a rowe.
Farewell, quod the olde man.
God kepe the, fayd the chylde than,
I take my leue at the;
God, that mooft beft may, 130
Kepe the bothe nyght and day.
Gramercy, fone, fayd he.
Than drewe it towarde the nyght,
Iacke hym hyed home full ryght,
It was his ordynaunce; 135
He toke his pype and began to blowe,
All his beeftes on a rowe,
Aboute hym they can daunce.
Thus wente he pypynge thrugh the towne,
His beeftes hym folowed by the fowne, 140
Into his faders clofe;
He wente and put them vp echone,
Homewarde he wente anone,
Into his faders hall he gofe.
His fader at his fouper fat, 145
Lytell Iacke efpyed well that,
And fayd to hym anone,
Fader, I haue kepte your nete,
I praye you gyue me fome mete,
I am an hongred, by Saynt Ihone: 150

I have fytten meteleffe
All this dayė kepynge your beeftes,
My dyner feble it was.
His fader toke a capons wynge,
And at the boye he gan it flynge,   155
And badde hym ete apace.
That greued his ftepmoders herte fore,
As I tolde you before,
She ftared hym in the face,
With that fhe let go a blafte,   160
That they in the hall were agafte,
It range ouer all the place.
All they laughed and had good game,
The wyfe waxed red for fhame,
She wolde that fhe had ben gone.   165
Quod the boye, well I wote,
That gonne was well fhote,
As it had ben a ftone.
Curfedly fhe loked on hym tho,
Another blafte fhe let go,   170
She was almooft rente.
Quod the boye, wyll ye fe
How my dame letteth pellettes fle,
In fayth or euer fhe ftynte?
The boye fayde vnto his dame,   175
Tempre thy bombe, he fayd, for fhame:
She was full of forowe.
Dame, fayd the good man, go thy waye,
For I fwere to the by my faye,
Thy gere is not to borowe,   . 180

Afterwarde as ye fhall here,
To the hous there came a frere,
To lye there all nyght;
The wyfe loued him as a faynt,
And to hym made her complaynt, 185
And tolde hym all aryght:
Wee haue a boye within ywys,
A fhrewe for the nones he is,
He dooth me moche care;
I dare not loke hym vpon, 190
I am afhamed, by Saynt Iohn,
To tell you how I fare:
I praye you mete the boy tomorowe,
Bete hym well and gyue hym forowe,
And make the boye lame. 195
Quod the frere, I fhall hym bete.
Quod the wyfe, do not forgete,
He dooth me moche fhame:
I trowe the boye be fome wytche.
Quod the frere, I fhall hym teche, 200
Haue thou no care;
I fhall hym teche yf I may.
Quod the wyfe, I the praye,
Do hym not fpare.
On the morowe the boye arofe, 205
Into the felde foone he gofe,
His beeftes for to dryue;

V. 186. *So* A. *and* MS. all *omitted in De W.*

The frere ranne out at the gate,
He was a ferde leeft he came to late,
He ranne faft and blyue. 210
Whan he came vpon the londe,
Lytell Iacke there he fonde,
Dryuynge his beeftes all alone;
Boye, he fayd, god gyue the fhame,
What haft thou done to thy dame? 215
Tell thou me anone:
But yf thou canft excufe the well,
By my trouth bete the I wyll,
I wyll no lenger abyde.
Quod the boye, what eyleth the? 220
My dame fareth as well as ye,
What nedeth ye to chyde?
Quod the boye, wyll ye wete
How I can a byrde fhete,
And other thynge withall? 225
Syr, he fayd, though I be lyte,
Yonder byrde wyll I fmyte,
And gyue her the I fhall.
There fate a byrde vpon a brere,
Shote on boy, quod the frere, 230
For that me lyfteth to fe.
He hytte the byrde on the heed,
That fhe fell downe deed,
No ferder myght fhe flee.

V. 211. *So* A. *and* MS. a londe. *De W.*

The frere to the buſhe wente, 235
Vp the byrde for to hente,
He thought it beſt for to done.
Iacke toke his pype and began to blowe,
Then the frere, as I trowe,
Began to daunce ſoone; 240
As ſoone as he the pype herd,
Lyke a wood man he fared,
He lepte and daunced aboute;
The breres ſcratched hym in the face,
And in many an other place, 245
That the blode braſt out;
And tare his clothes by and by,
His cope and his ſcapelary,
And all his other wede.
He daunced amonge thornes thycke, 250
In many places they dyde hym prycke,
That faſt gan he blede.
Iacke pyped and laughed amonge,
The frere amonge the thornes was thronge,
He hopped wunders hye; 255
At the laſt he held vp his honde,
And ſayd I haue daunced ſo longe,
That I am lyke to dye;

V. 255. A hoppyd wonderley hey;
    The boy ſeyde, and lowhe with all,
    Thes ys a ſport reyall,
    For a lord to ſe.   *MS. More.*

Gentyll Iacke, holde thy pype ftyll,
And my trouth I plyght the tyll,   260
I will do the no woo.
Iacke fayd, in that tide,
Frere fkyppe out on the ferder fyde,
Lyghtly that thou were goo.
The frere out of the bufshe wente,   265
All to ragged and to rente,
And torne on euery fyde;
Unnethes on hym he had one cloute,
His bely for to wrappe aboute;
His harneys for to hyde.   270
The breres had hym fcratched fo in the face,
And [in] many an other place,
He was all to bledde with blode;
All that myght the frere fe,
Were fayne awaye to flee,   275
They wende he had ben wode.
Whan he came to his hooft,
Of his iourney he made no booft,
His clothes were rente all;
Moche forowe in his herte he had,   280
And euery man hym dradde,
Whan he came in to the hall.
The wyfe fayd, where haft thou bene?
In an euyll place I wene,
Me thynketh by thyn araye.   285
Dame, I haue ben with thy fone,
The deuyll of hell hym ouercome,
For no man elles may.

With that came in the good man, 290
The wife fayd to hym than,
Here is a foule araye;
Thy fone that is the lefe and dere,
Hath almooft flayne this holy frere,
Alas! and welawaye! 295
The good man fayd, *benedicite!*
What hath the boye done frere to the?
Tell me without lette.
The frere fayd, the deuyll hym fpede,
He hath made me daunce, maugre my hede, 300
Amonge the thornes, hey go bette.*
The good man fayd to hym tho,
Haddeft thou loft thy lyfe fo,
It had ben grete fynne.
The frere fayd, by our lady, 305
The pype went fo meryly,
That I coude neuer blynne.
Whan it drewe towarde the nyght,
The boye came home full ryght,
As he was wont to do; 310
Whan he came into the hall,
Soone his fader gan hym call,
And badde hym to come hym to.

---

* *The name, it is probable, of fome old dance.* To " dance hey go mad" *is ftill a common expreffion in the North.*
V. 312, His fader dyde hym foone call. *De W.*

Boye, he fayd, tell me here,
What haft thou done to the frere ? 315
Tell me without lefynge.
Fader, he fayd, by my faye,
I dyde nought elles, as I you faye,
But pyped him a fprynge.
That pype, fayd his fader, wolde I here. 320
Mary, god forbede! fayd the frere;
His handes he dyde wrynge.
Yes, fayd the good man, by goddes grace.
Then, fayd the frere, out alas!
And made grete mournynge. 325
For the loue of god, quod the frere,
If ye wyll that pype here,
Bynde me to a poft;
For I knowe none other rede,
And I daunce I am but deed, 330
Well I wote my lyfe is loft.
Stronge ropes they toke in honde,
The frere to the pofte they bonde,
In the myddle of the halle;
All that at the fouper fat 325
Laughed and had good game therat,
And faid the frere wolde not fall.
Than fayd the good man,
Pype fonne, as thou can,
Hardely whan thou wylle. 340

V. 327. that he pype. *De W.*
V. 339. Pype on good fono. *Idem.*

Fader, he fayd, fo mote I the,
Haue ye fhall ynough of gle,
Tyll ye bydde me be ftyll.
As foon as Iacke the pype hent,
All that there were verament, 345
Began to daunce and lepe;
Whan they gan the pype here,
They myght not themfelfe ftere,
But hurled on an hepe.
The good man was in no dyfpayre, 350
But lyghtly lepte out of his chayre,
All with a good chere;
Some lepte ouer the ftocke,
Some ftombled at the blocke,
And fome fell flatte in the fyre. 355
The good man had grete game,
How they daunced all in fame;
The good wyfe after gan fteppe,
Euermore fhe keft her eye at Iacke,
And faft her tayle began to cracke, 360
Lowder than they coude fpeke.
The frere hymfelfe was almooft loft,
For knockynge his heed ayenft the poft,
He had none other grace;
The rope rubbed hym vnder the chynne, 365
That the blode downe dyde rynne,
In many a dyuers place.

V. 361. Lowde. *De W.*

Iacke ranne into the ſtrete,
After hym faſt dyde they lepe,
Truly they coude not ſtynte ; 370
They wente out at the dore ſo thycke,
That eche man fell on others necke,
So pretely out they wente.
Neyghbours that were faſt by,
Herde the pype go ſo meryly, 375
They ranne into the gate ;
Some lepte ouer the hatche,
They had no time to drawe the latche,
They wende they had come to late.
Some laye in theyr bedde, 380
And helde vp theyr hede,
Anone they were waked ;
Some ſterte in the waye,
Truly as I you ſaye,
Stark bely naked. 385
By that they were gadred aboute,
I wys there was a grete route,
Dauncynge in the ſtrete ;
Some were lame and myght not go,
But yet ywys they daunced to, 390
On handes and on fete.
The boye ſayd, now wyll I reſt.
Quod the good man, I holde it beſt,
With a mery chere ;

V. 392. They. *W.*

Seafe, fone, whan thou wylte, 395
In fayth this is the meryeſt fytte
That I herde this feuen yere.
They daunced all in fame,
Some laughed and had good game,
And fome had many a fall. 400
Thou curfed boye, quod the frere,
Here I fomon the that thou appere
Before the offycyall;
Loke thou be there on Frydaye,
I wyll the mete and I may, 405
For to ordeyne the forowe.
The boye fayd, by god auowe,
Frere, I am as redy as thou,
And Frydaye were to morowe.
Frydaye came as ye may here, 410
Iackes ſtepdame and the frere
Togeder there they mette;
Folke gadered a grete pafe,
To here euery mannes cafe,
The offycyall was fette. 415
There was moche to do,
Maters more than one or two,
Both with preeſt and clerke;
Some had teſtamentes for to preue,
And fayre women, by your leue, 420
That had ſtrokes in the derke.

V. 402, 403. Y fom' the affor the comfcrey. *MS.*

Euery man put forth his cafe,
Then came forth frere Topyas,
And Iackes ftepdame alfo;
Syr offycyall, fayd he,   425
I haue brought a boye to thee,
Which hath wrought me moche wo;
He is a grete nygromancere,
In all Orlyaunce is not his pere,
As by my trouth I trowe.   430
He is a wytche, quod the wyfe:
Than, as I fhall tell you blythe,
Lowde coude fhe blowe.
Some laughed without fayle,
Some fayd, dame, tempre thy tayle,   435
Ye wrefte it all amyffe.
Dame, quod the offycyall,
Tel forth on thy tale,
Lette not for this.
The wyfe was afrayed of an other cracke,   440
That no worde more fhe fpacke,
She durft not for drede.
The frere fayd, fo mote I the,
Knaue, this is long of the
That euyl mote thou fpede.   445
The frere fayd, fyr offycyall,
The boye wyll combre vs all,
But yf ye may him chafte;

V. 423. Than cam foret capias. *MS.*   *V.* 432. blyue. *A.*

Syr, he hath a pype truly,
Wyll make you daunce and lepe on hye, 450
Tyll your herte brafte.
The offycyall fayd, fo mot I the,
That pype wolde I fayne fe,
And knowe what myrth that he can make.

V. 453, That pype well y fe,
&c.   He feyde, boy, hes het her?
     Ye feer, be mey ffay,
     Anon pype ws a lay,
     And make vs all cher.
     The offeciall the pype hent,
     And blow tell his brow hen bent,
     Bot therof cam no gle;
     The offeciall feyde, this ys nowth,
     Be god that me der bowthe,
     Het ys not worthe a felo.
     Be mey fay, qod the freyr,
     The boy can make het pype cler,
     Y befcro hem for hes mede.
     The offeciall bad the boy a fay.
     Nay, qod the freyr, er that a way,
     For that y for bede.
     Pype on, qod the offeciall, and not fpar.
     The freyr began to ftar,
     Jake hes pype hent,
     As fone as Gake began to blow,
     All they lepyd on a rowe,
     And ronde abowt they went.

Mary, god forbede, than fayd the frere, 455
That he fholde pype here,
Afore that I hens the waye take.
Pype on, Iacke, fayd the offycyall,
I wyll here now how thou canft playe.
Iacke blewe vp, the fothe to faye, 460
And made them foone to daunce all.

  The offeciall had fo gret haft,
  That boyt hes fchenys braft,
  A pon a blokys hende.
  The clerkys to dans they hem fped,
  And fom all ther eynke fched,
  And fom ther bekes rent,
  And fom caft ther boky[s] at the wall,
  And fom ouer ther felowys can fall,
  So weytley they lepyd.
  Ther was withowt let,
  They ftombylled on a hepe,
  They danfed all a bowthe,
  And yever the freyr creyd owt,
  Y may no lengger dans for foyt,
  Y haffe loft halffe mey cod war,
  When y danfed yn the thornes.
  Som to crey they began,
  Mey boke ys all to toren;
  Som creyd withowt let,
  And fom bad hoo;
  Som feyde het was a god game,
  And fom feyde they wer lame,
  Y may no leynger fkeppe;

The offycyall lepte ouer the defke,
And daunced aboute wonder fafte,
Tyll bothe his fhynnes he all to breft,
Hym thought it was not of the beft,   465
Than cryed he vnto the chylde,
To pype no more within this place,
But to holde ftyll for goddes grace,
And for the loue of Mary mylde.

Som danfed fo long,
Tell they helde owt the townge,
And a nethe meyt hepe.
The offeciall began to ftar,
And feyde, hafe for they heyr,
Stent of they lay,
And boldeley hafke of me,
What thou welt hafe for thy gle,
Y fchall the redey pay.
Then to ftend Jake began,
The offeciall was a werey man,
Mey trowet y pleyt y the,
Thes was a god gle,
And feyde the worft that euer they fe,
For het was er neyth.
Then befpake the offeciall,
And leytley Gake can call,
Hes pype he hem hent,
And gaffe hem xx s.
And euer mor hes blefyng,
For that merey fet.

Than fayd Iacke to them echone, 470
If ye wolde me graunte with herte fre,
That he fhall do me no vylany,
But hens to departe euen as I come.
Therto they anfwered all anone,
And promyfed him anone ryght, 475
In his quarell for to fyght,
And defende hym from his fone,

When Gake had that money hent,
Anon homard he went,
Glad therof was he;
He waxed a wordeley marchande,
A man of gret degre.
Hes ftepdame, y dar fay,
Dorft neuer after that day,
Nat wonley ones defplefe.
They lowyd togedyr all thre,
Hes father, hes ftepdame and he,
Affter yn gret eys.
And that they ded, foyt to fay,
Tho hewyn they toke the way,
Withowtyn eney mes.
Now god that dyed for os all,
And dranke ayfell and gall,
Bryng them all to they bles,
That beleuet on the name Jh̄c.

Thus they departed in that tyde,
The offycyall and the fompnere,
His ftepdame and the frere,
With great ioye and moche pryde. 480

THE KING

AND

THE BARKER.

The following equally rude and ancient piece is given from the manuscript volume in the public library, Cambridge, already described. It is the undoubted original of " the merry, pleasant, and delectable history between K. Edward the fourth and a tanner of Tamworth," reprinted by Dr. Percy; who ought, perhaps, to have informed his readers that the old copies contain a great many stanzas which he has, not injudiciously, suppressed.

Dantre is Daventry (vulgarly pronounced Daintry), in Warwickshire.

The writer of the manuscript should seem to have been some provincial rustic. In one place of the volume he enters the following saw, which appeared worth preserving, for the sake of its singularity.

Ther ys leythe reythe and meythe,
Meythe ouerset reythe for the defawte of leythe,
Bot and reythe methe com to leythe,
Scholder neuer meythe ouerset reythe.

W ELL yow her a god borde to make yow
  ' all lawhe ?'
How het fell apon a tyme, or eney man het know,
The kyng rod a hontyng as that tyme was,
For to hont a der y trow hes hope was.
As he rode he houertoke yn the wey   5
A tannar of Dantre yn a queynte a raye;
Blake kow heydys fat he apon,
The hornys heyng befyde,
The kyng low and had god game,
To fe the tannar reyde.   10
Howr kyng bad hes men abeyde,
And he welde fper of hem the wey;

V. 1. lawhe all.

Yffe y may her eney new tythyng
Y fchall het to yow faye.
Howr kyng prekyd, and feyde, fer, god the faffe. 15
The tannar feyde, well mot yow ffar.
God felow, feyde 'howr' kyng, off on thyng y the pray,
To Drayton Bafet well y reyde, wyche ys the wey?
That can y tell the fro hens that y ftonde,
When thow comeft to the galow tre torne vpon the lyft honde.   20
Gramercy, felow, feyde owr kyng, withowtyn eney 'wone,'
I fchall prey they lord Bafet thanke the fone.
God felow, feyde owr kyng, reyde thou with me,
Tell y com to Drayton Bafet, now y het fe.
Nay be 'mey feyt' feyde the barker thoo,   25
Thow may fey y wer a fole and y dyd fo;
I haft yn mey wey as well as thow haft yn theyne,
Reyde forthe and feke they wey, thi hors ys better nar meyne.
The tanner feyde, what maner man ar ye?
A preker abowt, feyd the kyng, yn maney a contre. 30
Than fpake the thanner, foll fcredely ayen,
Y had a brother vowfed the fame
Tull he cowde never the.

V. 13. now.   *V.* 17. yowr.
V. 21. woyt.   *V.* 25. meyt.

Than 'howr' kyng fmotley gan fmeyle,
Y prey the felow reyde with me a meyle. 35
What devell, quod the tanner, art thou owt off they
   wet?
Y moft hom to mey deyner, for I am faftyng yet.
Good felow, feyde owr kyng, car the not for no
   mete,
Thou fchalt haffe mete ynow to neyzt, and yeffe thou
   welt ette.
The tanner toke gret fkorne of hem, 40
And fwar be creyft ys pync,
Y trow y hafe mor money in mey pors
Nar thow haft yn theyne :
Weneft thow y well be owt on neyzt? nay, and god
   be for,
Was y neuer owt a neyt fen y was bor. 45
The tanner lokyd a bake tho,
The heydes began to fall,
He was war of the keyngs men,
Wher they cam reydyng all.
Thes ys a theffe, thowt the tanner, 50
Y prey to god geffe hem car,
He well haffe mey hors,
Mey heydes, and all mey chaffar.
For feleyfchepe, feyde the tannar,
Yet wel y reyde with the ; 55
Y not war y methe with the afterward
Thow maft do as meche for me.

V. 34. yowr.

God a mar[fey], feyde owr kyng, withowt eny wone,
Y fchall prey the lord Bafet to thanke the fone.
Owr keyng feyde, what new tydyng hereſt as thou
   ryd ?   60
I wolde fayne wet for thow reydeſt weyde.
Y know now teytheyng, the thanner feyde, herke
   and thou fchalt here,
Off al the chaffar that y know kow heydys beyt der.
Owr keyng feyde, on theyng, as mey loffe y the prey,
What hereſt fey be the lord Bafet yn thes contrey ? 65
I know hem not, feyde the tanner, with hem y hafe
   lytyll to don,
Wolde he neuer bey of me clot lether to clowt ' his
   fchoyn.'
Howr kyng feyde, y loffe the well, of on thyng y
   the praye,
Thow haſt harde hes fervants fpeke, what welde
   they faye?
Ye for god, feyde the tanner, that tell y can,   70
Thay fey thay leke hem well, for he ys a god man.
Thos they reyd together talkyng, for foyt y yow
   tell,
Tull he met the lord Bafet, on kneys downe they fell.
Alas, the thanner thowt, the kyng ylone thes be,
Y fchall be hongyd, well y wot, at men may me fe. 75
He had no meynde of hes hode, nor cape ner adell,
Al for drede off hes leyffe he wende to halfe ler.

V. 60. now.   *V.* 67. with fchoys.

The thanner wolde aſtole awey,
Whyle he began to ſpeke,
Howr kyng had yever an ey on hem, 80
That he meyt not ſkape.
God felow, with me thow moſt abeyde, ſeyd owr
  kyng,
For thow and y moſt an hontyng reyde.
Whan they com to Kyng chas meche game they ſaye.
Howr kyng ſeyde, felow what ſchall y do, my hors
  ys ſo hey? 85
God felow, lend thow me theyne, and hafe her meyne.
Tho the tannar leyt done, and caſt a downe hes heydys;
Howr kyng was yn hes ſadell, no leyngger he beydes.
Alas, theyn the thanner thowt, he well reyde away
  with mey hors,
Y well after to get hem and y may. 90
He welde not leffe hes heydys beheynde for notheyng,
He caſt them yn the kyngs ſchadyll, that was a neys
  ſeyte;
Tho he ſat aboffe them, as y ouw ſaye,
He prekyd faſt after hem and fond the redey wey.
The hors lokyd abowt hem, and ſey on euery ſeyde 95
The kow hornes blake and wheyte;
The hors went he had bor the deuell on hes bake;
The hors prekyd as he was wode,
Het meſtoret to ſpor hem not;
The barker cleynt on hem faſt, 100
He was for a ferde for to fall,

The kyng lowhe, and was glad to folow the chas,
'Yette' he was agaſt leſt the tanner welde ber hem downe.
The hors ſped hem ſweythyli, he ſped hem wonderley faſt,
Ayen a bow of a noke the thanneres hed he barſt, 105
With a ſtombellyng as he rode the thanner downe he caſt;
The kyng lowhe and had god game, and ſeyde thou rydyſt to faſt.
The kyng lowhe, and had god game, and ſwar be ſent John,
Seche another horſman ſay y neuer none.
Owr kyng lowhe, and had god bord, and ſwar be ſent 'Jame,' 110
Y moſt nedyſt lawhe and thow wer mey dame.
Y be ſcro the fame ſon, ſeyde the barker tho,
That feche a bord welde haffe to ſe hes dame ſo wo.
When 'ther' hontyng was ydo, they changyd hors agen,
Tho the barker had hes howyn, theyrof he was 'fayne.' 115
Godamarſey, ſeyd our kyng, of they ſerueyſe to daye,
Yeffe thow hafe awt to do with me, or owt to ſaye,
They frende ſchall y yeffor be, be god that ys bet on.

V. 103. Yeffe.   *V.* 110. Jane.
V. 114. her.   *V.* 115. of fayne.

Godamarfey, feyde the barker tho, thow femyft a felow god,
Yeffe y met the yn Dantre thou fchalt dreynke be [the] rode. 120
Be mey feyt, feyde owr kyng, or els wer y to blame;
Yeff y met the yn Lecheffelde thou fchalt hafe the fame.
Thus they rod talkyng togeder to Drayton hall,
Tho the barker toke hes leffe of the lordes all.
Owr kyng comand the barker yn that tyde, 125
A C. s. yn hes pors to mend hes kow heydys.
Ther owr kyng and the barker partyd feyr a twyn .
God that fet yn heffen fo hey breyng os owt of fen!

HOW A MERCHANDE DYD HYS WYFE BETRAY.

The story of this ancient poem seems to have appeared in all possible shapes. It is contained in a tract intitled "Penny-wise, pound-foolish; or a Bristow diamond, set in two rings, and both crack'd. Profitable for married men, pleasant for young men, and a rare example for all good women," London, 1631. 4to. b.l. and is well known, at least in the North, by the old ballad called "The Pennyworth of Wit." It likewise appears, from Langhams Letter, 1575, to have been then in print, under the title of "The Chapman of a Pennyworth of Wit;" though no edition of that age is now known to exist. The following copy is from a transcript made by the late Mr. Baynes from one of Bp. Mores manuscripts in the public library at Cambridge (Ff. 2. 38, or 690), written apparently about the reign of Edward the fourth or Richard the third; carefully but unnecessarily examined with the original. The poem itself however is indisputably of a greater age, and seems from the language and orthography to be of Scotish, or at least of North country extraction. The fragment of a somewhat different copy, in the same dialect, is contained in a MS. of Henry the 6ths time in the British Museum (Bib. Har. 5396). It has evidently been designed to be sung to the harp.

Lysteny th, lordyngys, y you pray,
How a merchand dyd hys wyfe betray,
Bothe be day and be nyght,
Yf ye wyll herkyn aryght.
Thys fonge ys of a merchand of thys cuntre, 5
That had a wyfe feyre and free;
The marchand had a full gode wyfe,
Sche louyd hym trewly as hur lyfe,
What that euyr he to hur fayde,
Euyr fche helde hur wele apayde: 10
The marchand, that was fo gay,
By another woman he lay;

He boght hur gownys of grete pryce,
Furryd with menyvere and with gryfe,
To hur hedd ryall atyre, 15
As any lady myght defyre;
Hys wyfe, that was fo trewe as ſton,
He wolde ware no thyng vpon:
That was foly be my fay,
That fayrenes fchulde tru loue betray. 20
So hyt happenyd, as he wolde,
The marchand ouer the fee he fchulde;
To hys leman ys he gon,
Leue at hur for to tane;
With clyppyng and with kyffyng fwete, 25
When they fchulde parte bothe dyd they wepe.
Tyll hys wyfe ys he gon,
Leue at her then hath he tan;
Dame, he feyde, be goddys are,
Hafte any money thou woldyſt ware? 30
Whan y come bezonde the fee
That y myzt the bye fome ryche drewrè.
Syr, fche feyde, as Cryſt me faue,
Ye haue all that euyr y haue;
Ye fchall haue a peny here, 35
As ye ar my trewe fere,
Bye ye me a penyworth of wytt,
And in youre hert kepe wele hyt.
Styll ſtode the merchand tho,
Lothe he was the peny to forgoo, 40

Certen fothe, as y yow fay,
He put hyt in hys purce and yede hys way.
A full gode wynde god hath hym fende,
Yn Fraunce hyt can hym brynge;
A full gode fchypp arrayed he   45
Wyth marchaundyce and fpycerè.
Certen fothe, or he wolde refte,
He boght hys lemman of the befte,
He boght hur bedys, brochys and ryngys,
Nowchys of golde, and many feyre thyngys;
He boght hur perry to hur hedd,   51
Of fafurs and of rubyes redd;
Hys wyfe, that was fo trew as fton,
He wolde ware nothyng vpon:
That was foly be my fay,   55
That fayrenes fchulde trew loue betray.
When he had boght all that he wolde,
The marchand ouyr the fee he fchulde.
The marchandys man to hys mayfter dyd fpeke,
Oure dameys peny let vs not forgete. 60
The marchand fwore, be feynt Anne,
Zyt was that a lewde bargan,
To bye owre dame a penyworth of wytt,
In all Fraunce y can not fynde hyt.
' An' olde man in the halle ftode,   65
The marchandys fpeche he undurzode;

V. 65. And.

The olde man to the marchand can fay,
A worde of counfell y yow pray,
And y fchall felle yow a penyworth of wyt,
Yf ye take gode hede to hyt: 70
Tell me marchand, be thy lyfe,
Whethyr hafte thou a leman or a wyfe?
Syr, y haue bothe, as haue y refte,
But my paramour loue I befte.
Then feyde the olde man, withowten were, 75
Do now as y teche the here;
When thou comyft ouyr the falte fome,
Olde clothys then do the vpon,
To thy lemman that thou goo,
And telle hur of all thy woo; 80
Syke fore, do as y the fay,
And telle hur all thy gode ys lofte away,
Thy fchyp ys drownyd in the fom,
And all thy god ys lofte the from;
Whan thou hafte tolde hur foo, 85
Then to thy weddyd wyfe thou go;
Whedyr helpyth the bettur yn thy nede,
Dwelle with hur, as Cryfte the fpede.
The marchand feyde, wele muft thou fare,
Have here thy peny, y haue my ware. 90
When he come ouer the falte fome,
Olde clothys he dyd hym vpon,

VV. 79, 80. Thefe two lines are in the MS, inferted after the four following.

Hys lemman lokyd forthe and on hym fee,
And feyde to hur maydyn, how lykyth the?
My love ys comyn fro beyonde the fee,   95
Come hedur, and fee hym wyth thyn eye.
The maydyn feyde, be my fay,
He ys yn a febull array.
Go down, maydyn, in to the halle,
Yf thou mete the marchand wythalle,   100
And yf he fpyrre aftyr me,
Say, thou fawe me wyth non eye;
Yf he wyll algatys wytt,
Say in my chaumbyr y lye fore fyke,
Out of hyt y may not wynne,   105
To fpeke wyth none ende of my kynne,
Nother wyth hym nor wyth none other,
Thowe he were myn own brother.
Allas! feyde the maydyn, why fey ye foo?
Thynke how he helpyed yow owt of moche wo.
Fyrft when ye mett, wyth owt lefynge,   111
Youre gode was not worthe xx s.,
Now hyt ys worthe cccc pownde,
Of golde and fyluyr that ys rounde;
Gode ys but a lante lone,   115
Some tyme men haue hyt, and fome tyme none;
Thogh all hys gode be gon hym froo,
Neuyr forfake hym in hys woo.
Go downe, maydyn, as y bydd the,
Thou fchalt no lenger ellys dwelle wyth me.

The maydyn wente in to the halle, 121
There fche met the marchand wythall.
Where ys my lemman? where ys fche?
Why wyll fche not come fpeke wyth me?
Syr, y do the wele to wytt, 125
Yn hyr chaumbyr fche lyeth full fyke,
Out of hyt fche may not wynne,
To fpeke wyth non ende of hur kynne,
Nother wyth yow nor wyth non other,
Thowe ye were hur owne brother. 130
Maydyn, to my lemman that thou go,
And telle hur my gode ys lofte me fro,
My fchyp ys drownyd in the fom,
And all my gode ys lofte me from;
A gentylman have y flawe, 135
Y dar not abyde the londys lawe;
Pray hur, as fche louyth me dere,
As y have ben to hur a trewe fere,
To kepe me preuy in hur chaumbyr,
That the kyngys baylyes take me neuyr. 140
Into the chaumbyr the maydyn ys goon,
Thys tale fche tolde hur dame anone.
In to the halle, maydyn, wynde thou downe,
And bydd hym owt of my halle to goon,
Or y fchall fend in to the towne, 145
And make the kyngys baylyes to come;
Y fwere, be god of grete renown,
Y wyll neuyr harbur the kyngys feloun.

The maydyn wente in to the halle,
And thus fche tolde the merchand alle ;   150
The marchand fawe none other fpede,
He toke hys leve and forthe he yede.
Lyftenyth, lordyngys, curtes and hende,
For zyt ys the better fytt behynde.

[THE SECOND FIT.]

LYSTENYTH, lordyngys, great and fmall :
The marchand ys now to hys own halle ;
Of hys comyng hys wyfe was fayne,
Anone fche come hym agayne.
Hufbonde, fche feyde, welcome ye be,
How haue ye farde beyonde the fee ?   160
Dame, he feyde, be goddys are,
All full febyll hath be my fare ;
All the gode that euer was thyn and myn
Hyt ys lofte be feynt Martyn ;
In a ftorme y was beftadde,   165
Was y neuyr halfe fo fore adrad,
Y thanke hyt god, for fo y may,
That euyr y fkapyd on lyve away ;
My fchyp ys drownyd in the fom,
And all my gode ys lofte me from ;   170

A gentylman haue y flawe,
I may not abyde the londys lawe;
I pray the, as thou loueft me dere,
As thou art my trewe weddyd fere,
In thy chaumber thou woldeft kepe me dern.
Syr, fche feyde, no man fchall me warne: 176
Be ftylle, hufbonde, fygh not fo fore,
He that hathe thy gode may fende the more;
Thowe all thy gode be fro the goo,
I wyll neuyr forfake the in thy woo; 180
Y fchall go to the kyng and to the quene,
And knele before them on my kneen,
There to knele and neuyr to cefe,
Tyl of the kyng y haue getyn thy pees:
I can bake, brewe, carde and fpynne, 185
My maydenys and y can fylvyr wynne,
Euyr whyll y am thy wyfe,
To maynten the a trewe mannys lyfe.
Certen fothe, as y yow fay,
All nyght be hys wyfe he lay, 190
On the morne, or he forthe yede,
He kafte on hym a ryall wede,
And beftrode a full gode ftede,
And to hys lemmans hows he yede.
Hys lemman lokyd forthe and on hym fee, 195
As he come rydyng ouyr the lee,
Sche put on hur a garment of palle,
And mett the marchand in the halle,

Twyes or thryes, or euyr he wyſte,
Trewly ſche had hym kyſte.   200
Syr, ſche ſeyde, be ſeynt John,
Ye were neuyr halfe ſo welcome home.
Sche was a ſchrewe, as haue y hele,
There ſche currayed fauell well.
Dame, he ſeyde, be ſeynt John,   205
Zyt ar not we at oon;
Hyt was tolde me beyonde the ſee,
Thou haſte another leman then me,
All the gode that was thyn and myne,
Thou haſte geuyn hym, be ſeynt Martyn. 210
Syr, as Cryſte bryng me fro bale,
Sche lyeth falſely that tolde the that tale;
Hyt was thy wyfe, that olde trate,
That neuyr gode worde by me ſpake;
Were ſche dedd (god lene hyt wolde!)   215
Of the haue all my wylle y ſchulde;
Erly, late, lowde and ſtylle,
Of the ſchulde y haue all my wylle:
Ye ſchall ſee, ſo muſte y the,
That ſche lyeth falſely on me.   220
Sche leyde a canvas on the flore,
Longe and large, ſtyffe and ſtore,
Sche leyde theron, wythowten lyte,
Fyfty ſchetys waſchen whyte,
Pecys of ſyluyr, maſers of golde;   225
The marchand ſtode hyt to beholde:

He put hyt in a wyde fakk,
And leyde hyt on the hors bakk;
He bad hys chylde go belyue,
And lede thys home to my wyue.　　230
The chylde on hys way ys gon,
The marchande come aftyr anon;
He cafte the pakk downe in the flore,
Longe and large, ftyf and ftore,
As hyt lay on the grounde,　　235
Hyt was wele worthe cccc pownde:
They on dedyn the mouth aryght,
There they fawe a ryall fyght.
Syr, fayde hys wyfe, be the rode,
Where had ye all thys ryall gode?　　240
Dame, he feyde, be goddys are,
Here ys thy penyworth of ware;
Yf thou thynke hyt not wele befett,
Gyf hyt another can be ware hytt bett;
All thys wyth thy peny boght y,　　245
And therfore y gyf hyt the frely;
Do wyth all what fo euyr ye lyfte,
I wyll neuyr afke yow accowntys, be Cryfte.
The marchandys wyfe to hym can fay,
Why come ye home in fo febull array?　　250
Then feyde the marchand, fone ageyn,
Wyfe, for to affay the in certeyn;
For at my lemman was y before,
And fche by me fett lytyll ftore,

And fche louyd bettyr my gode then me, 255
And fo wyfe dydd neuyr ye.
To telle hys wyfe then he began,
All that gode he had takyn fro hys lemman;
And all was becawfe of thy peny,
Therfore y gyf hyt the frely;   260
And y gyf god a vowe thys howre,
Y wyll neuyr more have paramowre,
But the, myn own derlyng and wyfe,
Wyth the wyll y lede my lyfe.
Thus the marchandys care be gan to kele, 265
He lefte hys folye euery dele,
And leuyd in clenneffe and honeftè;
Y pray god that fo do we.
God that ys of grete renowne,
Saue all the gode folke of thys towne: 270
Jefu, as thou art heuyn kynge,
To the blys of heuyn owre foules brynge.

HOW THE WISE MAN TAUGHT HIS SON.

F

This little moral piece, which, for the time wherein it was written, is not inelegant, is given from a manuscript collection in the Harleian library in the British Museum (No. 1596), compiled in the reign of King Henry the sixth. It is not supposed to have been before printed, nor has any other copy of it been met with in manuscript; there is however a striking coincidence of idea in Mr. Gilbert Coopers beautiful elegy intitled " A father's advice to his son," as well as in the old song of " It's good to be merry and wise ;" which the more curious reader may consult at his leisure.

L YSTENYTH all, and ze well here
   How the wyfe man taght hys fon;
Take gode tent to thys matere,
   And fond to lere yf the con.
Thys fong be zonge men was begon,   5
   To make hem tyrfty and ftedfaft;
But zarn that is oft tyme yll fponne,
   Euyll hyt comys out at the laft.

A wyfe man had a fayre chyld,
   Was well of fyftene zere age,   10
That was bothe meke and mylde,
   Fayre of body and uefage;

HOW THE WISE MAN

Gentyll of kynde and of corage,
For he schulde be hys fadur eyre;
Hys fadur thus, yn hys langage,   15
' Taght' hys sone bothe weyll and fayre:

And sayd, son, kepe thys word yn hart,
And thenke theron ' tyll' thou be ded;
Zeyr day thy furst weke,
Loke thys be don yn ylke stede: 20
Furst se thye god yn forme of brede,*
And serue hym ' well' for hys godenes,
And afturward, sone, by my rede,
Go do thy worldys besynes.

Forst, worschyp thy god on a day,   25
And, sone, thys schall thou haue to ' mede,'
Skyll fully what thou pray,
He wyll the graunt with outyn drede,
And send the al that thou hast nede,
As ' far' as meser longyyth to strech, 30
This lyfe in mesur that thou lede,
And of the remlant thou ne rech.

And, sone, thy tong thou kepe also,
And be not tale wyse be no way,
Thyn owen tonge may be thy fo,   35
Therfor beware, sone, j the pray,

V. 16. That.   *V*. 18. thyll.   *V*. 22. wyll.
V. 26. mad.   *V*. 30. for.

* i. e. *go to mass.*

Where and when, fon, thou fchalt fay,
And be whom thou fpekyft oght;
For thou may fpeke a word to day
That feuen zere thens may be forthozt. 40

Therfore, fone, be ware be tyme,
Defyre no offys for to bere,
For of thy neyborys mawgref,
Thou moft hem bothe dyfplefe and dere,
Or ellys thy felf thou muft 'forfwere,' 45
And do not as thyn offys wolde,
And gete the mawgrefe here and there,
More then thank a thoufand fold.

And, fone, yf thou wylt lyf at efe,
And warme among thy neyburs fyt, 50
Lat newefangylnes the plefe
Oftyn to remewe nor to flyt,
For and thou do thou wantys wyt,
For folys they remewe al to wyde;
And alfo, fone, an euyl 'fygne' ys hyt, 55
A mon that can no wher abyde.

And, fone, of fyche thyng j the warne,
And on my blyffyng take gode hede,
Thou vfe neuer the tauerne;
And alfo dyfyng j the forbede: 60

V. 45. for fwete.   *V.* 55. fagne.

For thyfe two thyngys, with outyn drede,
    And comon women, as j leue,
Maks zong men euyle to fpede,
    And 'falle' yn danger and yn myfchefe.

And, fone, the more gode thou haft,   65
    The rather bere the meke and lowe;
Lagh not mych for that ys waft,
    For folys ben by laghing 'knowe.'
And, fone, quyte wele that thou owe,
    So that thou be of detts clere;   70
And thus, my lefe chylde, as j 'trowe,'
    Thou meft the kepe fro davngere.

And loke thou wake not to longe,
    Ne vfe not rere foperys to late;
For, were thy complexion neuyr fo ftrong, 75
    Wyth furfet thou mayft fordo that.
Of late walkyng oftyn debate,
    On nyztys for to fyt and drynke;
Yf thou wylt rule thyn aftate,
    Betyme go to bed and wynke.   80

And, fone, as far furth as thou may,
    On non enqueft that thou come,
Nor no fals wytneffe bere away,
    Of no manys mater, all ne fum:

V. 64. fulle.   *V.* 68. knone.   *V.* 71. trewe.

For better the were be defe and dowm, 85
  Then for to be on eny enqueſt,
That aftyr myzt be vndurnome,
  A trewe man had hys quarel left.

And, ſone, yf thou wylt haue a wyfe,
  Take hur for no couetyſe, 90
But loke, ſone, ſche be the lefe,
  Thou wyfe bywayt and wele awyſe,
That ſche be gode, honeſt, and wyſe,
  Thof ſche be pore take thou no hede,
For ſche 'ſchal' do the more ſeruys, 95
  Then ſchall a ryche with owtyn drede.

For better it is in reſt and pes,
  A mes of potage and no more,
Then for to haue a thouſand mes,
  With gret dyſeſe and angyr ſore. 100
Therfore, ſone, thynk on thys lore,
  Yf thou wylt haue a wyfe with eſe,
By hur gode ſet thou no ſtore,
  Thoffe ſche wolde the bothe feffe and ſeſſe.

And yf thy wyfe be meke and gode, 105
  And ſerue the wele and 'pleſantly,'
Loke that thou be not ſo wode,
  To charge hur then to owtragely;

V. 95. ſchalt.   *V*. 106. pleſantyl.

F 4

But then fare with hur efely,
  And cheryfch hur for hur gode dede,   110
For thyng ouerdon vnfkylfully,
  Makys wrath to grow where ys no nede.

I wyl neyther glos ne 'paynt,'
  But waran the on anodyr fyde,
Yf thy wyfe come to make pleynt,   115
  On thy feruandys on any fyde,
Be nott to hafty them to chyde,
  Nor wreth the or thou wytt the fothe,
For wemen yn wrethe they can not hyde,
  But fone they reyfe a fmokei rofe.   120

Nor, fone, be not jelows, j the pray,
  For, and thou falle in jelofye,
Let not thy wyfe wyt in no way,
  For thou may do no more foly;
For, and thy wyfe may onys afpye   125
  That thou any thyng hur myftryft,
In dyfpyte of thy fantefy,
  To do the wors ys all hur lyft.

Therfore, fone, j byd the
  Wyrche with thy wyfe as refon ys,   130
Thof fche be feruant in degre,
  In fom degre fhe felaw ys.

V. 113. praynt.

V. 118. *The MS. reads* wreth the not, *but the word* not *is inferted by a different, though very ancient, hand, which has corrected the poem in other places; and is certainly redundant and improper.*

Laddys that ar bundyn, fo haue j blys,
That can not rewle theyr wyves aryzt,
That makys wemen, fo haue j blys,　　135
To do oftyn wrong yn plyzt.

Nor, fone, bete nott thy wyfe j rede,
For ther yn may no help ' rife,'
Betyng may not ſtond yn ſtede,
But rather make hur ' the to defpyfe :'　140
Wyth louys awe, fone, thy wyfe chaſtyfe,
And let fayre wordys be thy zerde ;
Louys awe ys the beſt gyfe,
My fone, to make thy wyfe aferde.

Nor, fone, thy wyfe thou fchalt not chyde,
Nor calle hur by no vyleus name,　　146
For fche that fchal ly be thy fyde,
To calle hur fowle yt ys thy fchame ;
Whan thou thyne owen wyfe wyl dyffame,
Wele may anothyr man do fo :　　　150
Soft and fayre men make tame
Herte and buk and wylde roo.

And, fone, thou pay ryzt wele thy tythe *,
And pore men of thy gode thou dele ;
And loke, fone, be thy lyfe,　　　　155
Thou gete thy fowle here fum hele.

V. 135. *The latter half of this line feems repeated by miſtake.*
　　V. 138. be.　　　*V*. 140. to defpyfe the.
* *The author, from this and other admonitions, is fuppofed to have been a parfon.*

Thys werld hyt turnys euyn as a whele,
 All day be day hyt wyl enpayre,
And fo, fone, thys worldys wele,
 Hyt faryth but as a chery fare.   160

For all that euyr man doth here,
 Wyth befyneffe and trauell bothe,
All ys wythowtyn were,
 For oure mete, drynk, and clothe;
More getys he not, wythowtyn othe,   165
 Kyng or prynce whether that he be,
Be hym lefe, or be hym loth,
 A pore man has as mych as he.

And many a man here gadrys gode
 All hys lyfe dayes for othyr men,   170
That he may not by the rode,
 Hym felf onys ete of an henne;
But be he doluyn yn hys den,
 Anothyr fchal come at hys laft ende,
Schal haue hys wyf and catel then,   175
 That he has gadred another fchal fpende.

Therfor, fone, be my counfeyle,
 More then ynogh thou neuyr covayt,
Thou ne woft wan deth wyl the affayle,
 Thys werld ys but the fendys bayte.   180

V. 180. *The latter part of this ftanza feems to be wanting.*

For deth ys, fone, as I trowe,
　The moſt thyng that certyn ys,
And non ſo vncerteyn for to knowe,
　As ys the tyme of deth y wys;
And therfore ſo thou thynk on thys,　　　185
　And al that j haue feyd beforn:
And Iheſu ' bryng' vs to hys blys,
　That for us weryd the crowne of thorn.

V. 187. brynd.

THE LIFE AND DEATH

OF

TOM THUMBE.

It is needless to mention the popularity of the following story. Every city, town, village, shop, stall, man, woman, and child, in the kingdom, can bear witness to it. Its antiquity, however, remains to be enquired into, more especially as no very ancient edition of it has been discovered. That which was made use of on the present occasion bears the following title: " Tom Thumbe, his life and death: wherein is declared many maruailous acts of manhood, full of wonder, and strange merriments. Which little knight lived in king Arthurs time, and famous in the court of Great Brittaine. London, printed for John Wright. 1630." *It is a small* 8vo. *in black letter, was given, among many other curious pieces, by Robert Burton, author of the Anatomy of Melancholy, to the Bodleian Library* (Seld. Art. L. 79.), *and is the oldest copy known to be extant. There is a later edition, likewise in black letter, printed for F. Coles, and others, in Antony à Woods collection, which has been collated, as has also a different copy, printed for some of the same proprietors, in the editors possession. All three are ornamented with curious 'cuts, representing the most memorable incidents of our heros life. They are likewise divided into chapters by short prose arguments, which, being always unnecessary, and sometimes improper, as occasioning an interruption of the narrative, are here omitted.*

In Ben Jonsons Masque of the Fortunate Isles, designed for the Court, on the Twelfth Night, 1626,

Skelton, one of the characters, after mentioning Elinor Rumming, and others, says

> Or you may have come
> In, THOMAS THUMB,
> IN A PUDDING FAT,
> With Doctor Rat.

Then " The Antimasque follows: consisting of these twelve persons, Owl-glass, the four Knaves, two Ruffians, Fitz-Ale, and Vapor, Elinor Rumming, Mary Ambree, Long Meg of Westminster, TOM THUMB, and Doctor Rat." *

Five years before there had appeared " The History of Tom Thumbe, the Little, for his small stature surnamed, King Arthurs Dwarfe: Whose Life and aduentures containe many strange and wonderful accidents, published for the delight of merry Time-spenders. Imprinted at London for Tho: Langley, 1621, (12mo. bl.l.)" This however was only the common metrical story turned into prose with some foolish additions by R. I. [Richard Johnson.] The Preface or Introductory Chapter is as follows, being indeed the only part of the book that deserves notice.

" My merry Muse begets no Tales of Guy of Warwicke, nor of bould Sir Beuis of Hampton; nor wil. I trouble my penne with the pleasant glee of Robin

---

* Works, by Whalley, vi. 195. " Doctor Rat, the curate," is one of the Dramatis Personæ in " Gammar Gurtons Needle."

Hood, little Iohn, the Fryer and his Marian; nor will I call to minde the lusty Pindar of Wakefield, nor those bold Yeomen of the North, ADAM BELL, CLEM OF THE CLOUGH, nor WILLIAM OF CLOUDESLY, those ancient archers of all England, nor shal my story be made of the mad merry pranckes of Tom of Bethlem, Tom Lincolne, or Tom a Lin, the Diuels supposed Bastard, nor yet of Garagantua that monster of men*, but of AN OLDER TOM, A TOM OF MORE ANTIQUITY, a Tom of a strange making, I meane Little Tom of Wales, no bigger then a Millers Thumbe, and therefore for his small stature, surnamed Tom Thumbe..... The ANCIENT TALES of Tom Thumbe IN THE OLDE TIME, haue beene the only reuiuers of drouzy age at midnight; old and young haue with his Tales chim'd Mattens till the cocks crow in the morning; Batchelors and Maides with his Tales haue compassed the Christmas fire-blocke, till the Curfew-Bell rings candle out; the old Shepheard and the young Plow boy after their dayes labour, haue carold out a Tale of Tom Thumbe to make them merry with: and who but little Tom, hath made long nights seem short, and heauy toyles easie? Therefore (gentle Reader) considering that old modest mirth is turnd naked out of

---

* This is scarcely true; the titles of the two last chapters being, 1. "How Tom Thumbe riding forth to take the ayre, met with the great Garagantua, and of the speech that was betweene them." 2. "How Tom Thumbe after conference had with great Garagantua returned, and how he met with King Twadle."

doors, while nimble wit in the great Hall fits vpon a soft cushion giuing dry bobbes; for which cause I will, if I can, new cloath him in his former liuery, and bring him againe into the Chimney Corner, where now you must imagine me to fit by a good fire, amongst a company of good fellowes ouer a well spic'd Waffel-bowle of Christmas Ale telling of these merry Tales which hereafter follow." This is in the editors poffeffion.

In the panegyric verses (by Michael Drayton and others) upon Tom Coryate and his Crudities, London, 1611, 4to. our hero is thus introduced, along with a namesake, of whom, unfortunately, we know nothing further:

"TOM THUMBE is dumbe, vntill the pudding creepe,
"In which he was intomb'd, then out doth peepe.
"TOM PIPER is gone out, and mirth bewailes,
"He neuer will come in to tell vs tales."*

We are unable to trace our little hero above half a century further back, when we find him still popular, indeed, but, to our great mortification, in very bad company. " IN OUR CHILDHOOD (says honest Reginald Scot) our mothers maids haue so terrified vs with an ouglie diuell... and haue so fraied vs with bull beggers,

---

* In a different part of the work we find other characters mentioned, whose story is now, perhaps, irretrievably forgot:
I am not now to tell a tale
Of George a Green, or Iacke a Vale,
Or yet of Chittiface.

spirits, witches, vrchens, elues, hags, fairies, satyrs, pans, faunes, sylens, kit with the canslicke, tritons, centaurs, dwarfes, giants, imps, calcars, coniurors, nymphes, changlings, incubus, Robin good-fellow, the spoorne, the mare, the man in the oke, the helle waine, the fieredrake, the puckle, Tom Thombe, *hob-gobblin, Tom tumbler, boneles, and such other bugs, that we are afraide of our owne shadowes."* *

To these researches we shall only add the opinion of that eminent antiquary Mr. Thomas Hearne, that this History, " however looked upon as altogether fictitious, yet was CERTAINLY founded upon some AUTHENTICK HISTORY, as being nothing else, originally, but a description of KING EDGAR's DWARF." †

---

* *Discouerie of Witchcraft.* London, 1584, 4to. p. 155. See also Archb. Harsnets *Declaration of Popish Impostures.* Ibi. 1604, 4to. p. 135.

† Benedictus Abbas, Appendix ad Præfationem, p. LV. *Mr. Hearne was probably led to fix upon this monarch by some ridiculous lines added, about his own time, to introduce a spurious second and third part. See the common editions of Aldermary church-yard, &c. or that intitled* " Thomas Redivivus: or, a compleat history of the life and marvellous actions of Tom Thumb. In three tomes. Interspers'd with that ingenious comment of the late Dr. Wagstaff: and annotations by several hands. To which is prefix'd historical and critical remarks on the life and writings of the author." *London,* 1729. FOLIO. *Dr. Wagstaffs comment was written to ridicule that of Mr. Addison, in the Spectator, upon the ballad of Chevy-Chase, and is inserted in his Works.*

IN Arthurs court Tom Thumbe did liue,
   A man of mickle might,
The beſt of all the table round,
   And eke a doughty knight:

His ſtature but an inch in height,   5
   Or quarter of a ſpan;
Then thinke you not this little knight,
   Was prou'd a valiant man?

His father was a plow-man plaine,
 His mother milkt the cow, .   10
But yet the way to get a sonne
 ' This' couple knew not how,

Untill such time this good old man
 To learned Merlin goes,
And there to him his deepe desires   15
 In secret manner showes,

How in his heart he wisht to haue
 A childe, in time to come,
To be his heire, though it might be
 No bigger than his Thumbe.   20

Of which old Merlin thus foretold,
 That he his wish should haue,
And so this sonne of stature small
 The charmer to him gaue.

No blood nor bones in him should be,   25
 In shape and being such,
That men should heare him speake, but not
 His wandring shadow touch:

But so vnseene to goe or come
 Whereas it pleasd him still;   30
Begot and borne in halfe an houre,
 To fit his fathers will:

V. 12. these.

And in foure minutes grew fo faft,
  That he became fo tall
As was the plowmans thumbe in height, 35
  And fo they did him call

Tom Thumbe, the which the Fayry-Queene
  There gave him to his name,
Who, with her traine of Goblins grim,
  Vnto his chriftning came. 40

Whereas fhe cloath'd him richly braue,
  In garments fine and faire,
Which lafted him for many yeares
  In feemely fort to weare.

His hat made of an oaken leafe, 45
  His fhirt a fpiders web,
Both light and foft for thofe his limbes
  That were fo fmally bred;

His hofe and doublet thiftle downe,
  Togeather weau'd full fine; 50
His ftockins of an apple greene,
  Made of the outward rine;

His garters were two little haires,
  Pull'd from his mothers eye,
His bootes and fhooes a moufes fkin, 55
  There tand moft curiously.

Thus, like a luftie gallant, he
    Aduentured forth to goe,
With other children in the ftreets
    His pretty trickes to fhow.   60

Where he for counters, pinns, and points,
    And cherry ftones did play,
Till he amongft thofe gamefters young
    Had lofte his ftocke away.

Yet could he foone renue the fame,   65
    When as moft nimbly he
Would diue into ' their' cherry-baggs,
    And there ' partaker' be,

Unfeene or felt by any one,
    Vntill a fcholler fhut   70
This nimble youth into a boxe,
    Wherein his pins he put.

Of whom to be reueng'd, he tooke
    (In mirth and pleafant game)
Black pots, and glaffes, which he hung   75
    Vpon a bright funne-beame.

The other boyes to doe the like,
    In pieces broke them quite;
For which they were moft foundly whipt,
    Whereat he laught outright.   80

V. 67. the.   *V*. 68. a taker.

And fo Tom Thumbe reftrained was
   From thefe his fports and play,
And by his mother after that
   Compel'd at home to ftay.

Whereas about a Chriftmas time,   85
   His father a hog had kil'd,
And Tom 'would' fee the puddings made,
   'For fear' they fhould be fpil'd.

He fate vpon the pudding-boule,
   The candle for to hold;   90
Of which there is vnto this day
   A pretty paftime told:

For Tom fell in, and could not be
   For euer after found,
For in the blood and batter he   95
   Was ftrangely loft and drownd.

Where fearching long, but all in vaine,
   His mother after that
Into a pudding thruft her fonne,
   Inftead of minced fat.   100

Which pudding of the largeft fize,
   Into the kettle throwne,
Made all the reft to fly thereout,
   As with a whirle-wind blowne.

V. 87. to.   *V.* 88. Fear'd that.

For ſo it tumbled vp and downe,
    Within the liquor there,
As if the deuill 'had' been boyld;
    Such was his mothers feare,

That vp ſhe tooke the pudding ſtrait,
    And gaue it at the doore
Vnto a tinker, which from thence
    In his blacke budget bore.

But as the tinker climb'd a ſtile,
    By chance he let a cracke:
Now gip, old knaue, out cride Tom Thumbe,
    There hanging at his backe:

At which the tinker gan to run,
    And would no longer ſtay,
But caſt both bag and pudding downe,
    And thence hyed faſt away.

From which Tom Thumbe got looſe at laſt
    And home return'd againe:
Where he from following dangers long
    In ſafety did remaine.

Untill ſuch time his mother went
    A milking of her kine,
Where Tom vnto a thiſtle faſt
    She linked with a twine.

V. 107, had there.

A thread that helde him to the fame,
  For feare the bluftring winde   130
Should blow him thence, that fo fhe might
  Her fonne in fafety finde.

But marke the hap, a cow came by,
  And vp the thiftle eate.
Poore Tom withall, that, as a docke,   135
  Was made the red cowes meate:

Who being mift, his mother went
  Him calling euery where,
Where art thou Tom? where art thou Tom?
  Quoth he, Here mother, here: 140

Within the red cowes belly here,
  Your fonne is fwallowed vp.
The which into her fcareful heart
  Moft carefull dolours put.

Meane while the cowe was troubled much,
  In this her tumbling wombe,   146
And could not reft vntil that fhe
  Had backward caft Tom Thumbe:

Who all befmeared as he was,
  His mother tooke him vp,   150
To beare him thence, the which poore lad
  She in her pocket put.

Now after this, in fowing time,
    His father would him haue
Into the field to driue his plow,
    And therevpon him gaue   155

A whip made of a barly ſtraw,
    To driue the cattle on:
Where, in a furrow'd land new fowne,
    Poore Tom was loſt and gon.

Now by a raven of great ſtrength   160
    Away he thence was borne,
And carried in the carrions beake
    Euen like a graine of corne,

Unto a giants caſtle top,
    In which he let him fall,   165
Where foone the giant fwallowed vp
    His body, cloathes and all.

But in his belly did Tom Thumbe
    So great a rumbling make,
That neither day nor night he could 170
    The fmalleſt quiet take,

Untill the gyant had him ſpewd
    Three miles into the fea,
Whereas a fiſh foone tooke him vp
    And bore him thence away.   175

Which lufty fifh was after caught
  And to king Arthur fent,
Where Tom was found, and made his dwarfe,
  Whereas his dayes he fpent

Long time in liuely iollity,   180
  Belou'd of all the court,
And none like Tom was then efteem'd
  Among the noble fort.

Amongft his deedes of courtfhip done,
  His highneffe did command,   185
That he fhould dance a galliard braue
  Vpon his queenes left hand.

The which he did, and for the fame
  . The king his fignet gaue,
Which Tom about his middle wore   190
  Long time a girdle braue.

Now after this the king would not
  Abroad for pleafure goe,
But ftill Tom Thumbe muft ride with him,
  Plac't on his faddle-bow.   195

Where on a time when as it rain'd,
  Tom Thumbe moft nimbly crept
In at a button hole, where he
  Within his bofome flept.

And being neere his highneffe heart, 200
He crau'd a wealthy boone,
A liberall gift, the which the king
Commanded to be done,

For to relieue his fathers wants,
 And mothers, being old; 205
Which was fo much of filuer coyne
 As well his armes could hold.

And fo away goes lufty Tom,
 With three pence on his backe,
A heauy burthen, which might make 210
 His wearied limbes to cracke.

So trauelling two dayes and nights,
 With labour and great paine,
He came into the houfe whereas
 His parents did remaine; 215

Which was but halfe a mile in fpace
 From good king Arthurs court,
The which in eight and forty houres
 He went in weary fort.

But comming to his fathers doore, 220
 He there fuch entrance had
As made his parents both reioice,
 And he thereat was glad.

His mother in her apron tooke
　Her gentle fonne in hafte,　　　　　225
And by the fier fide, within
　A walnut fhell, him plac'd:

Whereas they feafted him three dayes
　Vpon a hazell nut,
Whereon he rioted fo long　　　　　230
　He them to charges put;

And there-upon grew wonderous ficke,
　Through eating too much meate,
Which was fufficient for a month
　For this great man to eate.　　　　235

But now his bufineffe call'd him foorth,
　King Arthurs court to fee,
Whereas no longer from the fame
　He could a ftranger be.

But yet a few fmall April drops,　　240
　Which fetled in the way,
His long and weary iourney forth
　Did hinder and fo ftay.

Until his carefull father tooke
　A birding trunke in fport,　　　　245
And with one blaft blew this his fonne
　Into king Arthurs court.

Now he with tilts and turnaments
  Was entertained so,
That all the best of Arthurs knights   250
  Did him much pleasure show.

As good Sir Lancelot of the Lake,
  Sir Tristram, and sir Guy;
Yet none compar'd with braue Tom Thum,
  For knightly chiualry.   255

In honour of which noble day,
  And for his ladies sake,
A challenge in king Arthurs court
  Tom Thumbe did brauely make.

Gainst whom these noble knights did run,   260
  Sir Chinon, and the rest,
Yet still Tom Thumbe with matchles might
  Did beare away the best.

At last sir Lancelot of the Lake
  In manly sort came in,   265
And with this stout and hardy knight
  A battle did begin.

Which made the courtiers all agast,
  For there that valiant man
Through Lancelots steed, before them all,   270
  In nimble manner ran.

Yea horſe and all, with ſpeare and ſhield,
  As hardly he was ſeene,
But onely by king Arthurs ſelfe
  And his admired queene,   275

Who from her finger tooke a ring,
  Through which Tom Thumb made way,
Not touching it, in nimble ſort,
  As it was done in play.

He likewiſe cleft the ſmalleſt haire   280
  From his faire ladies head,
Not hurting her whoſe euen hand
  Him laſting honors bred.

Such were his deeds and noble acts
  In Arthurs court there ſhowne,   285
As like in all the world beſide
  Was hardly ſeene or knowne.

Now at theſe ſports he toyld himſelfe
  That he a ſickneſſe tooke,
Through which all manly exerciſe   290
  He careleſly forſooke.

Where lying on his bed ſore ſicke,
  King Arthurs doctor came,
With cunning ſkill, by phyſicks art,
  To eaſe and cure the ſame.   295

His body being so slender small,
  This cunning doctor tooke
A fine prospective glasse, with which
  He did in secret looke

Into his sickened body downe,   300
  And therein saw that Death
Stood ready in his wasted guts
  To sease his vitall breath.

His armes and leggs consum'd as small
  As was a spiders web,   305
Through which his dying houre grew on,
  For all his limbes grew dead.

His face no bigger than an ants,
  Which hardly could be seene:
The losse of which renowned knight   310
  Much grieu'd the king and queene.

And so with peace and quietnesse
  He left this earth below;
And vp into the Fayry Land
  His ghost did fading goe.   315

Whereas the Fayry Queene receiu'd,
  With heauy mourning cheere,
The body of this valiant knight,
  Whom she esteem'd so deere.

For with her dancing nymphes in greene, 320
  She fetcht him from his bed,
With muficke and fweet melody,
  So foone as life was fled:

For whom king Arthur and his knights
  Full forty daies did mourne; 325
And, in remembrance of his name
  That was fo ftrangely borne,

He built a tomb of marble gray,
  And yeare by yeare did come
To celebrate the mournefull day, 330
  And buriall of Tom Thum.

Whofe fame ftill liues in England here,
  Amongft the countrey fort;
Of whom our wives and children fmall
  Tell tales of pleafant fport. 335

THE LOVERS QUARREL:

OR,

CUPIDS TRIUMPH.

This "*pleasant History,*" which "*may be sung to the tune of Floras Farewell,*" is here republished from a copy printed at London for F. Cotes and others, 1677, 12mo. bl. l. preserved in the curious and valuable collection of that excellent and most respected antiquary Antony à Wood, in the Ashmolean Museum; compared with another impression, for the same partners, without date, in the editors possession. The reader will find a different copy of the poem, more in the ballad form, in a Collection of "*Ancient Songs,*" published by J. Johnson. Both copies are conjectured to have been modernised, by different persons, from some common original, which has hitherto eluded the vigilance of collectors, but is strongly suspected to have been the composition of an old North country minstrel.

The full title is — "*The Lovers quarrel: or Cupids Triumph: being the pleasant history of Fair Rosamond of Scotland. Being daughter to the lord Arundel, whose love was obtained by the valour of Tommy Pots: who conquered the lord Phenix, and wounded him, and after obtained her to be his wife. Being very delightful to read.*"

OF all the lords in Scotland fair,
    And ladies that been fo bright of blee,
There is a noble lady among them all,
.   And report of her you fhall hear by me.

For of her beauty fhe is bright,   5
    And of her colour very fair,
She's daughter to lord Arundel,
    Approv'd his parand and his heir.

Ile fee this bride, lord Phenix faid,
    That lady of fo bright a blee,   10
And if I like her countenance well,
    The heir of all my lands fhe'ft be.

But when he came the lady before,
  Before this comely maid came he,
O god thee fave, thou lady fweet,   15
  My heir and parand thou fhalt be.

Leave off your fuit, the lady faid,
  As you are a lord of high degree,
You may have ladies enough at home,
  And I have a lord in mine own country;   20

For I have a lover true of mine own,
  A ferving-man of low degree,
One Tommy Pots it is his name,
  My firft love, and laft that ever fhall be.

If that Tom Pots [it] is his name,   25
  I do ken him right verily,
I am able to fpend fourty pounds a week,
  Where he is not able to fpend pounds three.

God give you good of your gold, fhe faid,
  And ever god give you good of your fee,   30
Tom Pots was the firft love that ever I had,
  And I do mean him the laft to be.

With that lord Phenix foon was mov'd,
  Towards the lady did he threat,
He told her father, and fo it was prov'd,   35
  How his daughters mind was fet.

O daughter dear, thou art my own,
    The heir of all my lands to be,
Thou shalt be bride to the lord Phenix,
    If that thou mean to be heir to me.   40

O father dear, I am your own,
    And at your command I needs must be,
But bind my body to whom you please,
    My heart, Tom Pots, shall go with thee.

Alas! the lady her fondness must leave,   45
    And all her foolish wooing lay aside,
The time is come, her friends have appointed,
    That she must be lord Phenix bride.

With that the lady began to weep,
    She knew not well then what to say,   50
How she might lord Phenix deny,
    And escape from marriage quite away.

She call'd unto her little foot-page,
    Saying, I can trust none but thee,
Go carry Tom Pots this letter fair,   55
    And bid him on Guildford-green meet me:

For I must marry against my mind,
    Or in faith well proved it shall be;
And tell to him I am loving and kind,
    And wishes him this wedding to see.   60

But fee that thou note his countenance well,
  And his colour, and fhew it to me;
And go thy way and high thee again,
  And forty fhillings I will give thee.

For if he fmile now with his lips,   65
  His ftomach will give him to laugh at the heart,
Then may I feek another true love,
  For of Tom Pots fmall is my part.

But if he blufh now in his face,
  Then in his heart he will forry be,   70
Then to his vow he hath fome grace,
  And falfe to him I'le never be.

Away this lacky boy he ran,
  And a full fpeed forfooth went he,
Till he came to Strawberry-caftle,   75
  And there Tom Pots came he to fee.

He gave him the letter in his hand,
  Before that he began to read,
He told him plainly by word of mouth,
  His love was forc'd to be lord Phenix bride.   80

When he look'd on the letter fair,
  The falt tears blemifhed his eye,
Says, I cannot read this letter fair,
  Nor never a word to fee or fpy.

My little boy be to me true, 85
 Here is five marks I will give thee,
And all thefe words I muft perufe,
 And tell my lady this from me :

By faith and troth fhe is my own,
 By fome part of promife, fo it's to be found, 90
Lord Phœnix fhall not have her night nor day,
 Except he can win her with his own hand.

On Guildford-green I will her meet,
 Say that I wifh her for me to pray,
For there I'le lofe my life fo fweet, 95
 Or elfe the wedding I mean to ftay.

Away this lackey-boy he ran,
 Then as faft as he could hie,
The lady fhe met him two miles of the way,
 Says, why haft thou ftaid fo long, my boy? 100

My little boy, thou art but young,
 It gives me at heart thou'l mock and fcorn,
Ile not believe thee by word of mouth,
 Unlefs on this book thou wilt be fworn,

Now by this book, the boy did fay, 105
 And Jefus Chrift be as true to me,
Tom Pots could not read the letter fair,
 Nor never a word to fpy or fee.

He fays, by faith and troth you are his own,
    By fome part of promife, fo it's to be found, 110
Lord Phenix fhall not have you night nor day,
    Except he win you with his own hand.

On Guildford-green he will you meet,
    He wifhes you for him to pray,
For there he'l lofe his life fo fweet,   115
    Or elfe the wedding he means to ftay.

If this be true, my little boy,
    Thefe tidings which thou telleft to me,
Forty fhillings I did thee promife,
    Here is ten pounds I will give thee.   120

My maidens all, the lady faid,
    That ever wifh me well to prove,
Now let us all kneel down and pray,
    That Tommy Pots may win his love.

If it be his fortune the better to win,   125
    As I pray to Chrift in trinity,
Ile make him the flower of all his kin,
    For the young lord Arundel he fhall be.

THE SECOND PART.

LET's leave talking of this lady fair,
   In prayers full good where she may be, 130
Now let us talk of Tommy Pots,
   To his lord and master for aid went he.

But when he came lord Jockey before,
   He kneeled lowly on his knee,
What news? what news? thou Tommy Pots, 135
   Thou art so full of courtesie.

What tydings? what tydings? thou Tommy Pots,
   Thou art so full of courtesie;
Thou hast slain some of thy fellows fair,
   Or wrought to me some villany. 140

I have slain none of my fellows fair,
   Nor wrought to you no villany,
But I have a love in Scotland fair,
   And I fear I shall lose her with poverty.

If you'l not believe me by word of mouth, 145
   But read this letter, and you shall see,
Here by all these suspitious words
   That she her own self hath sent to me.

But when he had read the letter fair,
  Of all the fuspitious words in it might be,   150
O Tommy Pots, take thou no care,
  Thou'ſt never lofe her with poverty.

For thou'ſt have forty pounds a week,
  In gold and filver thou fhalt row,
And Harvy town I will give thee,   155
  As long as thou intend'ſt to wooe.

Thou'ſt have forty of thy fellows fair,
  And forty horfes to go with thee,
Forty of the beſt ſpears I have,
  And I myfelf in thy company.   160

I thank you, maſter, faid Tommy Pots,
  That proffer is too good for me ;
But, if Jefus Chriſt ſtand on my fide,
  My own hands fhall fet her free.

God be with you, maſter, faid Tommy Pots,   165
  Now Jefus Chriſt you fave and fee ;
If ever I come alive again,
  Staid the wedding it fhall be.

O god be your fpeed, thou Tommy Pots,
  Thou art well proved for a man,   170
See never a drop of blood thou fpil,
  Nor yonder gentleman confound.

See that some truce with him thou take,
   And appoint a place of liberty;
Let him provide him as well as he can,   175
   As well provided thou shalt be.

But when he came to Guildford-green,
   And there had walkt a little aside,
There he was ware of lord Phenix come,
   And lady Rosamond his bride.   180

Away by the bride then Tommy Pots went,
   But never a word to her he did say,
Till he the lord Phenix came before,
   He gave him the right time of the day.

O welcome, welcome, thou Tommy Pots,   185
   Thou serving-man of low degree,
How doth thy lord and master at home,
   And all the ladies in that country?

My lord and master is in good health,
   I trust since that I did him see;   190
Will you walk with me to an out-side,
   Two or three words to talk with me?

You are a noble man, said Tom,
   And born a lord in Scotland free,
You may have ladies enough at home,   195
   And never take my love from me.

Away, away, thou Tommy Pots,
  Thou ferving-man ftand thou afide;
It is not a ferving-man this day,
  That can hinder me of my bride.   200

If I be a ferying-man, faid Tom,
  And you a lord of high degree,
A fpear or two with you I'le run,
  Before I'le lofe her cowardly.

Appoint a place, I will thee meet,   205
  Appoint a place of liberty,
For there I'le lofe my life fo fweet,
  Or elfe my lady I'le fet free.

On Guildford-green I will thee meet,
  No man nor boy fhall come with me.   210
As I am a man, faid Tommy Pots,
  I'le have as few in my company.

And thus ftaid the marriage was,
  The bride unmarried went home again,
Then to her maids faft did fhe laugh, 215
  And in her heart fhe was full fain.

My maidens all, the lady faid,
  That ever wait on me this day,
Now let us all kneel down,
  And for Tommy Pots let us all pray. 220

If it be his fortune the better to win,
 As I truſt to God in trinity,
Ile make him the flower of all his kin,
 For the young lord Arundel he ſhall be.

THE THIRD PART.

WHEN Tom Pots came home again, 225
 To try for his love he had but a week,
For ſorrow, god wot, he need not care,
 For four days that he fel ſick.

With that his maſter to him came,
 Says, pray thee, Tom Pots, tell me if thou doubt,
Whether thou haſt gotten thy gay lady, 231
 Or thou muſt go thy love without.

O maſter, yet it is unknown,
 Within theſe two days well try'd it muſt be,
He is a lord, I am but a ſerving man, 235
 I fear I ſhall loſe her with poverty.

I prethee, Tom Pots, get thee on thy feet,
 My former promiſes kept ſhall be;
As I am a lord in Scotland fair,
 Thou'ſt never loſe her with poverty. 240

For thou'ſt have the half of my lands a year,
  And that will raiſe thee many a pound,
Before thou ſhalt out-braved be,
  Thou ſhalt drop angels with him on the ground.

I thank you, maſter, ſaid Tommy Pots,   245
  Yet there is one thing of you I would fain,
If that I loſe my lady ſweet,
  How I'ſt reſtore your goods again?

If that thou win the lady ſweet,
  Thou mayſt well forth thou ſhalt pay me,   250
If thou looſeſt thy lady thou loſeſt enough,
  Thou ſhalt not pay me one penny.

You have thirty horſes in one cloſe,
  You keep them all both frank and free,
Amongſt them all there's an old white horſe   255
  This day would ſet my lady free;

That is an old horſe with a cut tail,
  Full ſixteen years of age is he;
If thou wilt lend me that old horſe,
  Then could I win her eaſily.   260

That's a fooliſh opinion, his maſter ſaid,
  And a fooliſh opinion thou tak'ſt to thee;
Thou'ſt have a better then ever he was,
  Though forty pounds more it ſhould coſt me.

O your choice horfes are wild and tough,   265
  And little they can fkill of their train;
If I be out of my faddle caft,
  They are fo wild they'l ne'r be tain.

Thou'ft have that horfe, his mafter faid,   270
  If that one thing thou wilt me tell;
Why that horfe is better then any other,
  I pray thee Tom Pots fhew thou to me.

That horfe is old, of ftomach bold,
  And well can he fkill of his train,   275
If I be out of my faddle caft,
  He'l either ftand ftill, or turn again.

Thou'ft have the horfe with all my heart,
  And my plate coat of filver free,
An hundred men to ftand at thy back,   280
  To fight if he thy mafter be.

I thank you mafter, faid Tommy Pots,
  That proffer is too good for me,
I would not for ten thoufand pounds
  Have man or boy in my company.   285

God be with you, mafter, faid Tommy Pots,
  Now as you are a man of law,
One thing let me crave at your hand,
  Let never a one of my fellows know.

I

For if that my fellows they did wot, 290
  Or ken of my extremity,
Except you keep them under a lock,
  Behind me I am sure they would not be.

But when he came to Guildford-green,
  He waited hours two or three, 295
There he was ware of lord Phenix come,
  And four men in his company.

You have broken your vow, said Tommy Pots,
  The vow which you did make to me,
You said you would bring neither man nor boy, 300
  And now has brought more than two or three.

These are my men, lord Phenix said,
  Which every day do wait on me;
If any of these dare proffer to strike,
  I'le run my spear through his body. 305

I'le run no race now, said Tommy Pots,
  Except now this may be,
If either of us be slain this day,
  The other shall forgiven be.

I'le make that vow with all my heart, 310
  My men shall bear witness with me;
And if thou slay me here this day,
  In Scotland worse belov'd thou never shalt be.

They turn'd their horses thrice about,
    To run the race so eagerly;   315
Lord Phenix he was fierce and stout,
    And ran Tom Pots through the thick o' th' thigh.

He bor'd him out of the saddle fair,
    Down to the ground so sorrowfully.
For the loss of my life I do not care,   320
    But for the loss of my fair lady.

Now for the loss of my lady sweet,
    Which once I thought to have been my wife,
I pray thee, lord Phenix, ride not away,
    For with thee I would end my life.   325

Tom Pots was but a serving-man,
    But yet he was a doctor good,
He bound his handkerchief on his wound,
    And with some kind of words he stancht his blood*.

He leapt into his saddle again,   330
    The blood in his body began to warm,
He mist lord Phenix body fair,
    And ran him through the brawn of the arm:

He bor'd him out of his saddle fair,
    Down to the ground most sorrowfully;   335
Says, prethee, lord Phenix, rise up and fight,
    Or yield my lady unto me.

* i e. *he made use of a charm for that purpose.*

Now for to fight I cannot tell,
    And for to fight I am not sure;
Thou haft run me throw the brawn o' the arm, 340
    That with a spear I may not endure.

Thou'ft have the lady with all my heart,
    It was never likely better to prove
With me, or any nobleman elfe
    That would hinder a poor man of his love. 345

Seeing you fay fo much, faid Tommy Pots,
    I will not feem your butcher to be,
But I will come and ftanch your blood,
    If any thing you will give me.

As he did ftanch lord Phenix blood, 350
    Lord! in his heart he did rejoice;
I'le not take the lady from you thus,
    But of her you'ft have another choice.

Here is a lane of two miles long,
    At either end we fet will be, 355
The lady fhall ftand us among,
    Her own choice fhall fet her free.

If thou'l do fo, lord Phenix faid,
    To lofe her by her own choice it's honefty,
Chufe whether I get her or go her without, 360
    Forty pounds I will give thee.

But when they in that lane was fet,
　The wit of a woman for to prove,
By the faith of my body, the lady faid,
　Then Tom Pots muft needs have his love.　365

Towards Tom Pots the lady did hie,
　To get on behind him haftily;
Nay ftay, nay ftay, lord Phenix faid,
　Better proved it fhall be.

Stay you with your maidens here,　　　370
　In number fair they are but three;
Tom Pots and I will go behind yonder wall,
　That one of us two be proved to dye.

But when they came behind the wall,
　The one came not the other nigh,　　375
For the lord Phenix had made a vow,
　That with Tom Pots he would never fight.

O give me this choice, lord Phenix faid,
　To prove whether true or falfe fhe be,
And I will go to the lady fair,　　　380
　And tell her Tom Pots flain is he.

When he came from behind the wall,
　With his face all bloody as it might be,
O lady fweet, thou art my own,
　For Tom Pots flain is he.　　　385

Now have I flain him, Tommy Pots,
    And given him deaths wounds two or three;
O lady fweet, thou art my own,
    Of all loves, wilt thou live with me?

If thou haft flain him, Tommy Pots,   290
    And given him deaths wounds two or three,
I'le fell the ftate of my fathers lands,
    But hanged fhall lord Phenix be.

With that the lady fell in a fwound,
    For a grieved woman, god wot, was fhe;   395
Lord Phenix he was ready then,
    To take her up fo haftily.

O lady fweet, ftand thou on thy feet,
    Tom Pots alive this day may be;
I'le fend for thy father, lord Arundel,   400
    And he and I the wedding will fee:

I'le fend for thy father, lord Arundel,
    And he and I the wedding will fee;
If he will not maintain you well,
    Both lands and livings you'ft have of me.   405

I'le fee this wedding, lord Arundel faid,
    Of my daughters luck that is fo fair,
Seeing the matter will be no better,
    Of all my lands Tom Pots fhall be the heir.

With that the lady began for to smile, 410
    For a glad woman, god wot, was she;
Now all my maids, the lady said,
    Example you may take by me.

But all the ladies of Scotland fair,
    And lasses of England, that well would prove, 415
Neither marry for gold nor goods,
    Nor marry for nothing but only love :

For I had a lover true of my own,
    A serving-man of low degree ;
Now from Tom Pots I'le change his name, 420
    For the young lord Arundel he shall be.

GLOSSARY.

ABRAIDE. *p.* 19. *The word at seems to be wanting:* At a braide; *at a push; at a start. It may, however, only mean* abroad.
Adrad. *p.* 75. *afraid.*
Algatys. *p.* 73. *by all means.*
Among. *p.* 132. *between.*
Amonge. *p.* 44. *(v.* 253.*) at the same time.*
And. *pp.* 28. 50. *an, if.*
Apayde. *p.* 69. *satisfyed, contented.*
Are. Goddys are. *pp.* 70. 76. *Gods heir or son,* i. e. *Jesus Christ, who is also God himself.*
Array. *p.* 73. *dress, clothing.*
Arrayed. *p.* 71. *freighted, furnished.*
Assay. Assaye. *p.* 27. *essay, try; p.* 79. *try, prove.*
Assoyld. *p.* 30. *absolved.*
A twyn. *p.* 65. *asunder.*
Auaunced. *p.* 30. *advanced, prefered.*
Auowe. *p.* 50. *a vow, an oath.*

Awyſe. *p.* 87.
Ayenſt. *p.* 48. *againſt.*
Bale. *pp.* 35. 78. *miſery, ſorrow, evil.*
Bargan. *p.* 71. *buſineſs, commiſſion.*
Barker. *pp.* 57, &c. *a tanner, ſo called from his uſing bark.*
Bedys. *p.* 71. *beads.*
Belyfe. *p.* 24. Belyue. *p.* 78. *immediately.*
Beſcro. *p.* 64. *beſhrew, curſe.*
Beſett, *p.* 78. *laid out, beſtowed.*
Beſtadde. *p.* 75. *ſituated, placed.*
Bett. *p.* 78. *better.* Ware hytt bett. *lay it out to more advantage.*
Bil. *p.* 18. *bill, an old Engliſh weapon, called a few lines before " a pollaxe."*
Blee. *p.* 117. *colour, complexion.*
Blynne. *p.* 46. *ſtop, ceaſe, give over.*
Blythe. *p.* 51. Blyue. *pp.* 26. 43. *blithe, with ſpirit.*
Boltes. *p.* 38. *arrows.*
Bor. *p.* 61. *born.*
Bord. Borde. *pp.* 60. 64. *jeſt.*
Borowe. *p.* 12. *bail, redeem, become pledges for.*
Bote. *p.* 21. *boot, remedy, advantage.*
Bowne. *p.* 24. *boon, favour.*
Braſte. *p.* 43. Braſte. *p.* 52. *burſt.*
Brede. *p.* 84. *bread.*
Bren. *p.* 10. Brenne. *p.* 9. *burn.*

GLOSSARY.

Brent. *p.* 10. *burnt.*
Breft. *pp.* 6. 9. 54. *burft, broke.*
Brochys. *p.* 71. *ornamental pins, or buckles, like the Roman* fibulæ, *(with a single prong) for the breaft or head-drefs.*
Bundyn. *p.* 89.
Bufke. *p.* 26. *bufked, addreffed, prepared, got ready.*
Bywayt. *p.* 87.
Chafte. *pp.* 36. 51. *chaftife, correct.*
Chaunce. Redy the juftice for to chaunce. *p.* 16. *This whole line feems a nonfenfical interpolation.*
Cheke. *p.* 39. *choaked.*
Chery fare. *p.* 90.
Clenneffe. *p.* 80. *cleannefs, chaftity.*
Clerk. *p.* 13. *fcholar.*
Cleynt. *p.* 63. *clung.*
Clyppyng. *p.* 70. *embracing.*
Comand. *p.* 65. *commanded, ordered.*
Combre. *p.* 51. *incumber, be too many for.*
Corage. *p.* 84. *heart, fpirit, inclination, difpofition.*
Curtes. *p.* 75. *courteous.*
Dame. *pp.* 74. 75. 77. *miftrefs.* Oure dameys peny. *p.* 71. *Our miftrefs's penny.*
Dampned. *p.* 12. *condemned.*
Den. *p.* 90. *grave.*

Dere. *p.* 85. *hurt.*
Dern. *p.* 76. *secret.*
Do gladly. *p.* 38. *eat heartyly.*
Doluyn. *p.* 90. *delved, buryed.*
Dongeon. *pp.* 11. 15. *prison. The prison in old castles was generally under-ground.*
Dradde. *p.* 45. *dreaded, feared.*
Drede. *pp.* 86. 87. *fear, doubt.*
Drewrè. *p.* 70. *The word properly signified love, courtship,* &c. *and hence a love-token, or love-gift; in which sense it is used by Bp. Douglas.*
Drough. *p.* 37. *drew.*
Dyd of. *p.* 14. *put off.*
Dyd on. *p.* 9. *put on.*
Euerechone. *p.* 6. Everichone. *p.* 23. Euerychone. *p.* 11. *every one.*
Eyre. *p.* 84. *heir.*
Eysell. *p.* 35. *vinegar.*
Fadur. *p.* 84. *v.* 15. *father. v.* 14. his fadur eyre, *his fathers heir.*
Fare, *p.* 6. *go.*
Fauell. *p.* 77. *deceit. See Skeltons* Bowge of Courte. *The meaning of the text is nevertheless still obscure, though it should seem to be the origin of our modern phrase* to curry favour.
Fay. *pp.* 29. 70. Faye. *pp.* 41. 47. *faith.*

GLOSSARY.

Fayne. *pp.* 8. 75. *fain, glad.*
Feble. *p.* 41. Febull. *p.* 73. Febyll. *p.* 76. *poor, wretched, miserable.*
Feche. *p.* 7. *fetch.*
Feffe. *p.* 87. *enfeof.*
Fere. *pp.* 6. 75. *wife. p.* 70. *husband. p.* 74. *lover, friend.*
Fet. *p.* 19. *fit, part, canto.*
Feyt. *pp.* 60. 65. *faith.*
Flyt. *p.* 85. *shift.*
Folys. *p.* 86. *fools.*
Fom. Fome. *p.* 72. *sea.*
Fond. *p.* 83. *endeavour, try.*
Fone. *p.* 55. *foes.*
Forbode. *p.* 29. *commandment.* Ouer Gods forbode. [Præter Dei præceptum sit.] q. d. *God forbid.* (PERCY.)
Fordo. *p.* 86. *undo, ruin, destroy.*
Forth. *p.* 128.
Forthozt. *p.* 85. *thought of, remembered.*
Forthynketh. *p.* 25. *grieveth, vexeth.*
Fosters. *p.* 26. *foresters.*
Fote. *p.* 7. *foot.*
Found. *p.* 7. *supported, maintained.*
Freke. *p.* 36. *fellow.*
Froo. *p.* 73. *from.*
Fyt. *p.* 12. Fytt. *p.* 75. *fit, part, canto.*
Fytte. *p.* 50. *strain.*

God. *p.* 72. *goods, merchandize.*
Godamarfey. *pp.* 62. 64. 65. *a corruption of* Gramercy. *See* Gramarcy.
Gode. *p.* 76. *goods, property.*
Goo. *p.* 76. *gone.*
Goon. *p.* 74. *go.*
Gramarcy. *pp.* 24. 38. 40. 60. *thanks,* grand mercie.
Greece. Hart of Greece. *p.* 21.
Gryfe. *p.* 70. *a species of fur.*
Gyfe. *p.* 89. *way, manner, method.*
Harowed. *p.* 14. *ravaged, ranfacked. Chrift went through hell as a conqueror, and plundered it of all the souls he thought worth carrying off.*
Hatche, *p.* 49. *a low or half door.*
Hedur. *p.* 73. *hither.*
Hele. *pp.* 77. 89. *health.*
Hem. *p.* 59. *him.*
Hende. *p.* 75. *civil, gentle.*
Hente. *p.* 44. *take.*
Hes. *p.* 59. *his.*
Het. *pp.* 59. 60. *it.*
Hie. *p.* 121. *go, run.*
High. *p.* 120. *hye, come, haften, return speedily.*
Hight. *p.* 5. *was called.*
Honge. *pp.* 12. 15. *hang, be hanged.*
Howr. *pp.* 59. 60. *our.*

GLOSSARY. 143

Howyn. *p.* 64. *own.*
Hye. *p.* 7. *go.*
Hyght. *p.* 39. *promised.*
Hyne. *p.* 35. *a* hind *is a servant.*
Kele. *p.* 79. *cool.*
Kneen. *p.* 76. *knees.*
Kynd. *p.* 84. *nature.*
Lagh. *p.* 86. *laugh.*
Laghing. *p.* 86. *laughing.*
Lante. *p.* 73. *lent.*
Launde. *p.* 21. *plain, open part of a forest.*
Leace. *pp.* 21. 22. *lyes, lying, doubt.*
Leasynge. *p.* 25. *lying, falsehood, doubt.*
Lee. *p.* 77. *plain, open field.*
Lefe. *p.* 24. *agreeable.* that is the lefe. *p.* 46. *that is so dear to thee; whom thou art so fond of. pp.* 86. 87. *dear, or beloved.* Be hym lefe, or be hym lothe. *p.* 90. *Let him like it or not; let him be agreeable or unwilling.*
Leffe. *p.* 65. *leave.*
Leman. *pp.* 70. 72. Lemman. *pp.* 71. 72. 73. *mistress, concubine. p.* 78. *lover, gallant, paramour.*
Lene. *p.* 78. *v.* 215. *lend.*
Lenger. *p.* 12. *longer.*
Lere. *p.* 83. *learn.*
Lesynge. *pp.* 25. 47. 73. *lying, falsehood.*

Lette. *p.* 46. *delay.* Lette not for this. *p.* 51. *be not hindered or prevented by what has happened from proceeding.*

Letteth. *p.* 19. *let, hinder, prevent.*

Leue. *p.* 86. *believe.*

Leuer. *pp.* 10. 24. 25. *rather, sooner.*

Lewde. *p.* 71. *foolish.*

Lightile. *pp.* 11. 12. *quickly.*

Linde. *p.* 20. *the linden or lime tree; a tree in general.*

Lith. *p.* 6. *incline, attend.*

Lordeyne. *p.* 14. *fellow.* Not, as foolishly *supposed, from* Lord Dane, *but from* lourdin *or* falourdin, *French.*

Lordyngys. *p.* 69, &c. *firs, masters, gentlemen.*

Lore. *p.* 87. *doctrine.*

Lough. *p.* 19. *laugh. p.* 39. *laughed.*

Loves. Of all loves. *p.* 134. *an adjuration frequently used by Shakspeare and contemporary writers.*

Low. *p.* 59. *laughed.*

Lowde and ſtylle. *p.* 78. *windy and calm; foul and fair;* i. e. *in all seasons; at all times.*

Lowhe. *p.* 64. *laughed.*

Lowſed. *p.* 17. *let go, let fly.*

Luſt. *p.* 37. *deſire, inclination.*
Lyghtly. *pp.* 7. 14. 19. &c. Lyghtlye. *p.* 18. *quickly, nimbly.*
Lynde. *p.* 19. *See* Linde.
Lyſt. *p.* 88. *inclination, deſire.*
Lyſtenyth. *p.* 69. *liſten.*
Lyte. *pp.* 37. 39. 43. *little.*
Lyue. *p.* 38. *life.*
Maſers. *p.* 77. *drinking cups.*
Maugre. *p.* 46. *in ſpite of.*
Maugref. Mawgrefe. *p.* 85. *ill-will.*
Mayſtry. More mayſtry. *p.* 27. *ſomething in a more maſterly or capital ſtile; a ſtill cleverer thing.*
Mede. *p.* 84. Meed. *p.* 8. *reward.*
Menyvere. *p.* 70. *a ſort of fur.*
Meſtoret. *p.* 63. *needed.*
Met. *pp.* 28. 65. *meet, meted, meaſured.*
Meteleſſe. *p.* 41. *meatleſs, without meat.*
Meyny. *p.* 19. *aſſembly, multitude.*
Mo. *p.* 26. *more.*
Mote. *p.* 7. *might; pp.* 36. 37. 48. 51. *may.*
Mought. *p.* 20. *might.*
Myrthes. *p.* 6. *pleaſant paſſages, merry adventures.*
Nar. *p.* 60. *nor, than.*
Nete. *pp.* 36. 40. *cows, horned cattle.*
Neys. *p.* 63. *nice, fine.*
Nones. *p.* 42. *occaſion.*

K

Nowchys of golde. *p. 71. ornaments for a womans dress; but not certain whether necklaces or hair pins.*

Nygromancere. *p..51. necromancer.*

Offycyal. *p. 50, &c. the commissary or judge of a bishops court.*

On dedyn. *p. 78. undid, untyed.*

On lyue. *p. 75. alive.*

Oon. Not at oon. *p. 77. Not at one, not friends.*

Ordynaunce. *p. 40. enjoined or regular practice.*

Other. *p. 36. either.*

Out horne. *p. 18. summoning horn, horn blown (as if to arms) in time of danger.*

Paramour, *p. 72.* Paramowre. *p. 79. mistress, concubine.*

Parand. His parand and his heir. *p. 117. his heir apparent.* My heir and parand. *p. 118. my heir apparent.*

Pay. *p. 24. satisfaction.*

Pees. *p. 76. peace, pardon.*

Perry. *p. 71. jewels, precious stones.*

Plyght. *pp. 39. 45. pledge, give.*

Plyzt. *p. 89. plight, condition.*

Prece. Inprece. *p. 10. in a press, in a croud, in a throng.*

Preced. *p. 18. pressed, thronged; p. 22. pressed forward.*

Preker. *p.* 60. *rider.*
Prekyd. *p.* 60. *rode up*; *p.* 63. *rode.*
Preftly. *p.* 22. *readyly, quickly.*
Preue. *p.* 50. *prove.*
Pryme. *pp.* 6. 16. *morning;* " *The firft quarter of the artificial day.*" (TYRWHITT.)
Pyne. *p.* 61. *pain, torment.*
Quarel. *p.* 87. *caufe, fuit.*
Queft. *p.* 15. *inqueft, jury.*
Quod. *pp.* 41. 42. *quoth, faid.*
Quyte. *p.* 86. *quit, pay, difcharge.*
Rech. *p.* 84. *reck, care for.*
Rede. *p.* 47. 84. *advice, counfel*; *p.* 88. *advife.*
Remewe. *p.* 85. *remove.*
Renne. *p.* 10. *run.*
Rere foperys. *p.* 86. *after-fuppers.*
Rewth. *p.* 25. *ruth, pity.*
Rode. *p.* 36. Rood. *p.* 74. *crofs.*
Ryall. *p.* 70. *royal, magnificent.*
Ryfed. *p.* 8. *raifed, caufed to rife.*
Saffe. *p.* 60. *fave.*
Safurs. *p.* 71. *fapphires.*
Same. All in fame. *p.* 48.
Saye. *p.* 63. *faw.*
Sayne. *pp.* 36. 37. *fay.*
Schrewe. *p.* 77. *fhrew, wicked or curfed one.*
Scredely. *p.* 60. *fhrewdly.*

Se. *p.* 20. *seen;* *p.* 37. *see, regard, superintend, keep in sight.*
Sen. *p.* 61. *since.*
Sesse. Feffe and sesse. *p.* 87. *enfeof and seise,* sub. *in house or land.*
Sheene. *p.* 12.
Shent. Make officers shent. *p.* 22. *cause them to be reprimanded.*
Shete. *pp.* 38. 43. *shoot.*
Shot window. *p.* 8. *a window that opens and shuts.*
Shrewe. *p.* 42. *wicked or cursed one.*
Slawe. *pp.* 74. 76. *slain.*
Smotley. *p.* 61. *pleasantly.*
Sompnere. *p.* 56. *summoner or apparitor; an officer who serves the summonses or citations of the spiritual court.* See *Chaucers* Canterbury Tales.
Sothe. *pp.* 71. 88. *truth.*
Sowne. *p.* 40. *sound.*
Soyt. *p.* 62. *soth, sooth, truth.*
Sper. *p.* 59. Spyrre. *p.* 73. *ask, enquire.*
Spercles. *p.* 10. *sparks (of fire).*
Spycerè. *p.* 71. *spices.*
State. *p.* 134. *estate.*
Stere. *pp.* 39. 40. *steer, rule, govern.*
Sterte. *p.* 17. *started, flew.* Sterte in the waye. *p.* 49. *started, rushed hastily, flew into the street.*

GLOSSARY. 149

Store. *p.* 77. *p.* 78. *v.* 234. *ſtrong*; *p.* 78. *v.* 254. *value.*
Stound. *p.* 15. *hour, time.*
Stowre. *p.* 18. *fight.*
Stynte. *p.* 49. *ſtay.*
Suſpitious. *pp.* 123. 124. *ſignificant.*
Sweythyli. *p.* 64. *ſwiftly.*
Syke. *p.* 72. *ſigh.*
Syth. *p.* 9. *ſince.*
Tan. *p.* 70. *taken.*
Tane. *p.* 70. *take.*
Teene. *p.* 12. *grief, ſorrow.*
Tempre. *pp.* 41. 51. *correct, manage.*
Tent. *p.* 83. *heed.*
The. *pp.* 48. 51. 60. 77. *thrive.*
Tho. *pp.* 26, &c. *then.*
Throng. *p.* 13. *ran.*
To. *p.* 16. *two.*
Trate. *p.* 77. *trot, hag.*
Trew mannys lyfe. *p.* 77. *the life of an honeſt man.*
Trewe man. *p.* 87. *honeſt man.*
Tyrſty. *p.* 83. *truſty.*
Undurnome. *p.* 87. *taken up, received, or entertained (as a notion).*
Undurzode. *p.* 66. *underſtood.*
Unnethes. *p.* 45. *ſcarcely.*
Verament. *pp.* 37. 48. *truly.*

Villany. *p.* 123. *mischief, injury.*
Vowfed. *p.* 60.
Voyded. *p.* 17. *avoided, withdrew, made off, got out of the way.*
Vylany. *p.* 55. *mischief, injury.*
Vyleus. *p.* 89. *vile, villainous, shameful.*
Waran. *p.* 88. *warn.*
Ware. *p.* 70. *expend, lay out.*
Ware. *p.* 72. *purchase.*
Warne. *p.* 76. *prevent, hinder.*
Wede. *pp.* 44. 76. *coat, cloak, dress, attire, clothing.*
Weke. Thy furſt weke. *p.* 84. *at thy firſt waking; as ſoon as thou wakeſt.*
Wend. *p.* 30. *go.*
Wende. *pp.* 6. 10. 20. 49. *weened, thought.*
Were. *p.* 90.
Wet. *p.* 62. Wete. *p.* 43. *know.*
Wight. *p.* 12. *ſtrong.*
Wis. *p.* 21. *think, take it.*
Wode. *pp.* 45. 87. *mad.*
Wone. *pp.* 60. 62. *hesitation.*
Wood. *p.* 44. *mad.*
Woſt. *p.* 90. *wotest, knoweſt.*
Wreſte. *p.* 51. *turn.* Wreſte it all amyſſe; *turn it the wrong way: a metaphor from tuning the harp.*

GLOSSARY.

Wreth. *p.* 88.
Wyght. *p.* 19. *strong.*
Wyle. *p.* 13. *feint, device, trick.*
Wynde. *p.* 74. *wend, go.*
Wynke. *p.* 86. *sleep.*
Wynne. *p.* 76. *earn, get;* *pp.* 73. 74. *get, come.*
Wyrche. *p.* 88. *work, conduct thyself.*
Wys. *pp.* 36. 49. *trow, think.*
Wyste. *p.* 77. *knew, was aware.*
Wyt. *p.* 88. *know.*
Wyte. *p.* 37. *blame.*
Wytt. *pp.* 73. 88. *know.* Do the wele to wytt. *p.* 74. *let thee perfectly know.*
Y. *pp.* 36, &c. *I.*
Y do. *p.* 64. *done.*
Yede. *pp.* 71. 75. 76. *went.*
Yeffe. *pp.* 64. 65. *if.*
Yeffor. *p.* 64. *ever.*
Yong men. *p.* 19. Yonge men. *p.* 12. *Yeomen.* See Spelmanni Glossarium, vv. Juniores, Yeoman.
Yslaw. *p.* 25. *slain.*
Ywys. *pp.* 42. 49. *I trow, I know.*
Zarn. *p.* 83. *yarn.*
Ze. *p.* 83. *ye.*
Zerde. *p.* 83. *rod.*

Zere. *p.* 83. *years.*
Zeyr day. *p.* 84.
Zonge. *p.* 83. *young.*
Zyt. *pp.* 71. 75. *yet.*

www.ingramcontent.com/pod-product-compliance
Lightning Source LLC
Chambersburg PA
CBHW030245170426
43202CB00009B/635